To
Our Dear Son
+ wife
Gloria
"
"We love you"
Mother Daddy
July 8, 1987

TRIUMPH OVER TERROR ON FLIGHT 847

TRIUMPH OVER TERROR ON FLIGHT 847

CAPT.
JOHN TESTRAKE
With DAVID J. WIMBISH

Fleming H. Revell Company
Old Tappan, New Jersey

ISBN 8007-1527-6

Copyright © 1987 by John Testrake
Published by the Fleming H. Revell Company
Old Tappan, New Jersey 07675
Printed in the United States of America

ROBERT D. STETHEM
United States Navy
Patriot—Christian

In the predawn hours of 15 June 1985,
on the airport runway at Beirut, Lebanon,
Robert Stethem gave his life for his country.
He looked at hate and death squarely and fearlessly,
and no cry was heard to come from him.
He stood alone that night in that faraway place
for you and for me—his countrymen.
I am honored to be called his fellow American.
Captain John Testrake

Contents

Be strong and of good courage, do not fear or be in dread of them: for it is the Lord your God who goes with you; he will not fail you or forsake you.

Deuteronomy 31:6 RSV

1

The Calm Before the Storm

The sky was a clear, deep blue—and breezes floating in off the Saronic Gulf made it an absolutely delightful day. It was the sort of morning that made you feel good just to be alive, and I felt a special joy welling up within me as I looked across the table at the petite, golden-haired beauty sitting across from me—my wife, Phyllis.

Phyllis and I would be celebrating our eighth anniversary in five days, and we were both looking forward to our anniversary cruise among the Greek islands.

Neither one of us had any inkling that our lives were about to be drastically interrupted. Later that day—June 14, 1985—I would be flying out of Athens as the captain of TWA Flight 847, on a relatively short trip to Rome. There was no sign, not even an ominous cloud in the sky, to indicate that I would be flying, not to Rome, but into a seventeen-day ordeal in the bowels of terrorist insanity.

Phyllis and I were enjoying a leisurely breakfast on the terrace of our hotel room. Athens has hundreds of shops where one can buy oranges, dates, and various types of delicious pastries for breakfast, or cold cuts and cheeses for lunch. We liked to sit out on the terrace, overlooking the city, and just enjoy being alone together in this beautiful, historic place.

I took another glance at my watch and quickly drained my second cup of coffee.

"Looks like it's about time for me to go."

Phyllis nodded.

I stood up, pushing my chair away from the table, walked around, and gave Phyllis a good-bye hug.

"Okay," I reminded her, "I'm going to Rome this morning, and then I'll be back through this afternoon on my way to Tel Aviv." I leaned over and kissed her cheek.

"Then tomorrow I'll pass through on my way down to Cairo."

Phyllis took my hands in hers. "You have a good trip. And I'll see you in a couple of days."

"Listen," I said, "I've got an idea. Why don't we see about your going to Cairo with me tomorrow?"

"That would be great, if you—"

"When I get to the airport, I'll check the passenger list. I'll give you a call this afternoon and let you know if there's space available."

Having Phyllis along on the trip to Cairo would be an extra anniversary present for both of us. Phyllis didn't know that the last time I'd been in Cairo I had gone to the bazaar and picked out a beautiful gold necklace and bracelet combination as her anniversary present. I was already looking forward to giving it to her, imagining the delighted sparkle in her eyes.

I kissed her good-bye, snatched my bag up from the bed, and walked out the door, like any businessman going off to an un-eventful day at the office.

The other members of the crew were already gathering in the

hotel lobby. There were my first officer, Phil Maresca, and flight engineer, Christian Zimmermann. I had met both of them just the night before.

Phyllis and I had run into Maresca and Zimmermann at the hotel and had asked them to join us for dinner. Zimmermann declined, as he had already made plans for the evening, but Maresca took us up on our offer.

We discovered that Phil is a native New Yorker who now makes his home in Salt Lake City because he loves to ski. He's a bachelor, a rugged outdoorsman, and Phyllis and I both knew immediately that we liked him. He told us that he was a last-minute addition to Flight 847, as he needed one more flight to fulfill his monthly quota.

In our brief conversations with Christian we learned that he had been in Europe for the past month, and that this would normally be his off-duty time. Instead, he had been asked to fill in for another flight engineer who needed time off to deal with a family matter.

It was interesting that none of the three of us were supposed to be on Flight 847. As for me, even though I was originally scheduled to serve as captain on that flight, the airline had asked me, just days before, if I would mind switching to a later flight, as a matter of convenience in scheduling.

Usually, when the airline asked me to make a switch like that, I wanted to do anything I could to help out. But this time Phyllis and I had plans for our anniversary, and I wasn't about to change them for anyone. Or so I thought!

Also present in the hotel lobby was the purser, Uli Derickson, and her four flight attendants, none of whom I had met before. We introduced ourselves all around and then climbed into the waiting crew bus for the short trip to the airport.

I should interject here that it is not unusual for flight crews to meet for the first time just prior to flying together. TWA trains its people very rigorously so that crew members are interchangeable. The high, strict standards make it possible for different crew members to work together without any loss of efficiency. Each crew member knows exactly what is expected of him and goes about doing that job.

On the way to the airport, there was no time for chitchat or for getting to know one another better. Uli Derickson pretty much dominated the conversation, because she was briefing her flight attendants regarding the order of service once the flight was under way. She had everything organized, down to the smallest detail, and I was impressed with her professional manner and efficiency.

Once we arrived at the airport, the purser and the flight attendants went their way, while Maresca, Zimmermann and I went down to the ready room in the basement.

Christian was there only long enough to ascertain the fuel load for the trip to Rome, and then he headed out to the aircraft. Meanwhile, Phil and I scanned the teletype for weather reports and checked out other information regarding our flight.

The weather looked good all along the route.

"Ought to have a clear shot into Rome," Phil said.

"It's about time!" I answered. The weather over Italy had been lousy for the last two months.

About half an hour before departure time, Phil and I took our bags and headed for the airplane. We found Christian already at his station, and the passengers were boarding.

I told Uli that the weather ahead looked good and reported on our estimated flying time to Rome.

Then Phil and I went on into the cockpit, sat down in our seats, checked our oxygen masks, and began getting things ready for the flight. I asked Christian for a quick report on the condition of the aircraft, and he informed me that everything checked out fine. Then, while Phil was getting out his charts, I began flipping switches to make sure everything was operating properly.

Then it was time for the final preflight check:

"Gear lever and lights?" Phil asked.

"Down and check," I replied.

"Brakes?" he continued.

"Parked."

"Flight instruments?"

"Checked."

"Radios?"

"On and check."

And so on through the rest of the checklist.

The ticket agent stuck his head in the door and told us that everyone was on board.

"Are you all ready to go?"

"Ready," I answered.

"Okay! You have a good trip, and I'll see you this afternoon."

As he walked out, closing the door behind him, the mechanic's voice came over the radio. "Clear to start engines."

Phil immediately got on the radio with the tower, asking for permission to start the engines.

Once that was granted, I fired them up in sequence: number one, number two, and number three—the engines roared to life.

"We have three good starts," I reported to the mechanic on the ground below.

"Stand by for hand signals," came his reply.

One last check of the equipment with the engineer—and then, following the mechanic's salute, I eased the airplane out of the parking stand and began rolling down the taxiway.

Normally, you could expect to sit at the end of the runway for some time awaiting airways clearance. But today, everything seemed to be going in our favor. There wasn't as much traffic as usual, and our wait was a short one.

We would be taking off toward the north, over a highly developed residential area. Once we were in the air, we would pick up a radio signal from Athens. We'd ride that out until we picked up the nondirectional beacon from Corinth, which would guide us across the Saronic Gulf, over Corinth, and on toward Corfu.

Normal procedure after takeoff is to climb steeply at 250 knots until reaching ten thousand feet, then to shallow the climb rate and accelerate to normal climb speed. This minimizes the time spent by high-performance jet aircraft in the slower, lightplane environment.

However, European lightplane traffic is practically nonexistent in many areas, and this rule is frequently waived. In this case, since the air was smooth and there was no traffic in the area, I had asked for and received permission to make a high-speed climb.

Because of the flatter climb angle, the flight attendants could also get a quicker start on their service rounds—and I knew from hearing Uli talk to her crew that the service on this flight was a complicated, lavish affair.

As we began climbing above the city of Athens, I banked away from the airport to keep from flying over the residential areas and headed west.

Looking down, I could see the cruise ships and other craft dotting the sparkling blue waters of the bay. It truly was a picture-postcard morning.

We were only a few minutes into the flight, no higher than four-to-five thousand feet, when I reached up and slipped off the Fasten Seatbelts sign. *Might as well let the girls get started with their service,* I thought.

Almost immediately, there was a banging sound in the cabin behind us.

At first, I thought it was merely the sound of the flight attendants getting out their service carts, because there is quite a bit of noise when the carts are taken out of storage.

But this noise was different, and it kept up. I quickly realized that whatever it was, it was more than just the service carts.

"What's that noise?" I asked.

"I don't know," Christian replied. "I'll check it."

He got up and looked through the peephole in the door that separates the cockpit from the cabin.

He looked for only a couple of seconds, before he pulled his face away from the door.

Very quietly and calmly he said, "We've got a hijack."

The nightmare had begun.

Learning to Fly

It doesn't seem possible that I've been flying airplanes for TWA for more than thirty years, in one capacity or another. It's an old cliché that "time flies when you're having fun." But it must be true, because I love flying, and the years have certainly rushed by for me.

But when I think back to the airliners of the 1950s and see how far we've come, then I realize that, yes, it has been a long time. Today's sleek jets make the propeller-driven aircraft of thirty years ago seem like covered wagons by comparison.

Still, it is hard for me to realize that I will soon be sixty years old—and that means I'll have to retire. It won't be easy stepping aside, because I love flying so much. I'll continue to fly my little private plane, but I'll miss being at the controls of a 747 or a Lockheed L-1011, bound for New York or Paris or Bombay.

The closer I get to it, the more ridiculous the age-sixty mandatory retirement looks. But then there are dozens of well-qualified younger men and women who are anxious for their time in the captain's seat, and the only way they'll ever get the chance they deserve is for older fellows, like me, to step aside.

When I do step aside, one thing is certain. I'll have enough memories to last me for the next sixty years.

I grew up in western New York State, at a time when the world was huge and the Middle East might as well have been 10 million miles away. I never dreamed that I would one day become a pawn in an international game of chess, nor that this incident would thrust me into the public eye. The limelight was something I studiously avoided as a youngster.

I was gangly, awkward, and shy—a country boy who didn't feel that he fit in well with the town kids from nearby Ripley.

My grandfather had come to this country from Holland, indenturing himself as a hired hand until he could pay off his boat fare across the Atlantic. But in time, he had been able to buy land along the Lake Erie shore, where he grew grapes.

My father was his eldest son. When he was twenty-one he married my mother and bought a fifty-seven-acre farm just half a mile away from my grandfather's place. My dad began planting grapes on his land and it was there, in 1927, that I was born.

The depression hit just as my parents were trying to get established, so things were definitely not easy. We were desperately poor, but so was everyone else. In fact, because we owned land, we had it better than some of the people who lived in town. We didn't have any money or a car, and we never had any new clothes. But at least we could grow our own food—we had a huge garden and some dairy cows—so we were able to get by.

I compensated for my shyness, and what I saw as my lack of

18

popularity, by escaping into adventure books. I read constantly—books about faraway, exotic places where men built bridges, hunted tigers, sailed square-riggers, or flew over ice caps.

Then when I was twelve years old, I fell in love for the first time. When my father took my brother and me to the little grass airport in Ripley and bought us a five-dollar plane ride, I entered into what has been a lifetime love affair with aviation.

As we soared above the houses of Ripley and over the nearby fields, and I saw the sun glinting off the surface of Lake Erie, I knew that someday I would be a pilot.

From that day on, my adventure books took a distant second place in my life. Aviation was my reason for living. I built model airplanes, dozens—hundreds—of them, and I read any book I could find that had to do with flying.

It got so bad that the model airplanes were taking over my bedroom. Finally, my mother couldn't take it any longer: "No more!" she scolded me. "Enough is enough. You find something better to do with your time!"

By that time there were so many model airplanes around the house she must have thought they were like rabbits—multiplying on their own.

But Mom couldn't stop me. When the order came to cease and desist, I merely moved my airplane factory into the barn. There, in the loft above the granary, I could build model airplanes to my heart's content—and Mom didn't even have to know about it.

When World War II broke out, all of the men who ordinarily did the farm work had other, more urgent business to take care of. Most of them went into the military. Others, like my father, went to work in the defense plants.

Dad was hired at the generous sum of twenty-five dollars per week.

I'll never forget the day he came home with his first week's paycheck. We all thought twenty-five dollars was a handsome salary indeed, especially since it would be paid every week. Farming in the depression had never been like this!

Eventually, Dad saved enough to buy a tractor, and because he wasn't available to run it himself, I did. I also began contracting my services out to neighboring farmers. During the day, I was enrolled in Ripley High School. After school and on weekends, I was usually perched upon that tractor.

But my heart was never in farming. I still wanted to fly. And I knew that as soon as I could, that's what I would be doing.

Like most of the guys at Ripley High, I was anxious to get into the service, to see some action before the war was over. And I intended to serve my country in the cockpit of a B-17 or a P-38.

Unfortunately for me, I had an astigmatism. Because of that, I was turned down when I tried to enroll in a cadets' program. I even tried to enlist as an aerial gunner, but discovered, to my chagrin, that a gunner has to have good eyes, too. Again, I was turned down.

So when high school graduation arrived, in June of 1945, instead of heading off to war, I found myself working in a packing plant. I was bored, restless, and perhaps a bit angry over my failure to become a Flying Ace.

My career in the packing plant didn't last long, though. One day the boss was on my back about something or other, and I came back at him with a smart reply. As a result, he told me in no uncertain terms to take the rest of my life off.

But I didn't go home. Instead, I went to the highway, stuck out my thumb, and hitched the thirty or so miles to Jamestown, where the nearest navy recruiting station was located. The place was run by a salty old chief petty officer who had gold stripes and hash marks all the way from his shoulder to his cuff. I told him I wanted to enlist for a six-year hitch, the longest term available.

He looked at me for a few seconds without saying anything, then he sat back, rubbed his chin, and said, "Son, I don't think you want to do that.

"I'll put you down for three years!"

So the adventure had begun. I was in the navy. I'd be having a life of excitement and danger, living out some of the stories I had read in those adventure books many years before.

But before any of that could happen, it was discovered that I had taken typing in high school. So I hadn't even gotten through boot camp, when I was sent to Washington to work in the Navy Department, typing reports. There I was, straight off the farm, a seaman second class, walking the halls of the Pentagon with the likes of Admirals Halsey and Nimitz.

I would often see them pass by, ablaze with gold braid and trailed by their huge contingents of aides and marine guards—and that was about the only excitement I got!

Pounding a typewriter in Washington wasn't exactly the adventure I had planned. I wanted action, and more than that, I was still hoping that the navy could get me involved in aviation.

Finally, when I couldn't take the frustration any longer, I typed up a florid, passionate request for a transfer to sea duty. I then took the request to my chief petty officer boss, to get his reaction.

His response was to throw up his hands in horror—not at my request, but because of the way I had written it.

"No! No! No!" he yelled. "That's not the way you do that!"

He rolled a piece of paper into his typewriter and pounded out my request in proper, formal, dispassionate military style. It was about three sentences in its entirety, compared with my three-page masterpiece.

I was disappointed, to say the least, because I had spent hours drafting a request that absolutely reeked with passionate idealism. And I couldn't bring myself to give all that up and replace it with his bland, unfeeling document. So I went back to my desk and typed up a new transfer request—a compromise between my original and my boss's rewrite. That did the job.

When asked what I wanted to do at sea, I replied that it didn't matter, just as long as it had to do with airplanes. A week later,

I found myself on an aircraft carrier—a part of the Sixth Fleet in the middle of the Mediterranean.

My job was up on the flight deck, working with the colorfully dressed crews who move the airplanes around the deck. I found out quickly that it's no simple task to conduct aircraft-carrier operations. It was an exciting, dangerous life.

Sometimes an airplane would hit the deck and burn. Sometimes it would slide across the deck and go over the side. At other times the hydraulic catapults then in use would malfunction, giving a "bad shot." The aircraft being launched, instead of soaring into the air, would fall into the sea ahead of the ship. If he was lucky, the pilot would swim free of the sinking plane and the rushing hull and bob in the boiling wake until picked up by a trailing destroyer. I, myself, was working within inches of the invisible propellers.

Still, the danger was something I quickly came to accept. I can't say that I ever really got used to seeing people killed or hurt, but I eventually came to accept the danger as a part of the job. And I was happy because I was as close as I had ever been to flying.

When my stint of sea duty was over, I was sent to Jacksonville, Florida, and then to San Francisco, where I watched the huge Martin Mars flying boats arrive each day from their glamorous trans-Pacific runs.

In 1948, when my hitch was up, I decided to attend Spartan School of Aeronautics in Tulsa. My initial plan was to attend the college there and earn a degree in aeronautical engineering. I discovered to my dismay that I had missed by two days on my enlistment date the changeover from wartime to peacetime GI Bill entitlement rules and had only half the credit I had anticipated. As a second choice I enrolled in aircraft and engine mechanic school. I planned to use this training in Alaska, where I had heard there was a fortune to be made working with the bush pilots. So, in the winter of 1949, I climbed aboard my motorcycle and headed for Oklahoma.

Not long after my arrival in Tulsa, I met a slender, dark-eyed beauty named Patricia. She was the most wonderful human being I had ever met, and suddenly—for the first time in my life—aviation was relegated to second place on my list of priorities.

Patricia was a sweet, Christian girl—a Methodist who attended church just about every time the doors were open. Her family belonged to a large, active church with a vibrant youth program. And because I wanted to be with Patricia, I became regular in my church attendance as well. I didn't take seriously most of what I heard at church. Oh, I believed there was a God out there—somewhere. But I didn't believe that any one religion had all the answers, and I mistrusted the Bible. My attitude was that it was just an old book, and why should I believe that the people who wrote it knew any better than anyone else?

I remembered the time when I was in the navy, on leave from the ship in Norfolk, Virginia, when a man on the street had invited me to a USO program that turned out to be sponsored by local Christians. He had given me a pocket New Testament. I thanked him for it, then dropped it in the bottom of my seabag and just forgot about it, thinking that I didn't have time to spend reading it.

Still, I liked going to church and being part of the fellowship—even if I told myself it was just because I liked being with Patricia.

My stay in Tulsa was extended when, at about the time I was finished with the aircraft-mechanic training, the school announced a brand-new course for airline flight engineers. Pan Am had been using flight engineers on its long-range flying boats, and TWA was using them on Boeing Stratoliners and Lockheed Constellations, which were just then coming into service. But then, the Federal Aviation Administration passed a new rule that any civilian airliner weighing more than eighty thousand pounds must have a flight engineer. That included the Douglas DC-6 and all large airliners built after that.

I still had some credit left on the GI Bill, so I decided to use it on this new training program. Besides, there was a recession going on, and there were no jobs to be found anywhere. My best friend, Bob Wilson, and I decided that we would both enroll in the flight-engineer program.

Unfortunately, when that training ended, the nation's economic situation still had not improved all that much. So Bob and I wound up working as airplane mechanics at a small grass airport just outside of Tulsa. There we would wait for the big job offers to come along.

The job definitely wasn't much. It paid only $125 per month, but it also provided a place to sleep—the owner of the airport set up two army cots in the hangar. For our meals, Bob and I would fix hot dogs and hamburgers over a hot plate, so it wasn't costing us very much to live. The major drawback of the job, as far as I was concerned, was that I didn't have enough money to take Patricia out on dates.

Much of our time together was spent at her house—talking or listening to the radio. We also spent time out at the airport or exploring on my motorcycle. By that time she and I were engaged. We were very much in love and planned to be married just as soon as I could afford it.

Then the Korean War came along, and a young man who kept his airplane parked at our airport was drafted. He owned a war surplus Fairchild PT-19 primary trainer, which had never been licensed as a civilian airplane. In fact, it still carried the star insignia and the air force serial number on its tail.

It could not legally be flown this way and so had little value. The owner asked if Bob and I would buy it. We offered him fifty dollars and a parachute for it, and he took it. To our surprise, we discovered that the plane was in excellent condition. In fact, it had put in only forty hours of flying time since it had left the factory.

All Bob and I had to do was give the plane a complete inspection, sign it off as being airworthy, process the necessary paperwork for a civilian registration, and, presto, we were the proud owners of an airplane. The main expense for the whole operation was an elaborate five-color paint job.

24

I learned to fly in that airplane. Our boss had been a B-29 bomber pilot during the war, and every evening he would take me up for an hour or so in our brand-new Fairchild. Sitting behind the controls in one of the plane's two open cockpits was everything I'd always dreamed it would be—and more.

When I was flying, I felt at peace with myself and the rest of the world. I felt the same excitement I had felt as a boy of twelve, when my father splurged and took my brother and me on that short flight from the Ripley airport.

I was happy, and I knew good things were headed my way. That was confirmed by a telegram from American Airlines. They wanted me to come to work for them as a DC-6 flight engineer. All of my schooling was about to pay off. One by one, my goals were being fulfilled.

But a funny thing happened on my way to American Airlines.

I was at Patricia's house one night, on one of our typical "dates," and we were reading the newspaper.

We had read all of the important stories and were way back about page 13 or so.

Suddenly, Patricia's eye caught something.

"Why, that's your name!" she exclaimed.

"Where?"

"Right here!"

She pointed at a little article in the center of the page. The entire article was less than an inch long.

"It says you've been recalled to active duty!"

"What?"

I couldn't believe it, but it was true. I was being called back into the navy.

When I left the navy I had joined the reserves, thinking it would be a good way to supplement my income. But after signing up, I discovered that the Tulsa area didn't have an opening for my classification and therefore couldn't pay me. When that happened, I simply stopped going to the meetings and lost touch with the other guys in the reserves. I hadn't seen any of them for more than a year!

Our date ended on a somewhat sour note that night, and the next morning, the first thing I did was to call the reserve office and ask what was going on.

"What's this thing I read in the Tulsa paper?" I asked.

"It's true," answered the voice on the other end. "You'd better get on down here and see about it."

When I got there, the officer in charge seemed totally surprised to see me. He had his nose buried in paperwork and didn't notice me when I first walked in.

I cleared my throat to get his attention.

He peered up at me over his glasses.

"Testrake? Where in the world have you been?"

"Right here. Working at the local airport."

"Really? We thought you were back in Illinois somewhere."

I knew then that if I hadn't happened to see that tiny little article, there was no way they would have been able to track me down. I could have had my job with American Airlines if I had just kept my mouth shut!

It's not that I wasn't patriotic, or that I didn't want to serve my country. But I felt I had already put in my time. I was launched in a new career and didn't want to back up.

I told everybody who would listen—and a few who wouldn't listen—that I couldn't go back into the navy, because I had a flying job offer from American Airlines.

"Well, that's tough," I was told, over and over again, "but you have to go back into the navy!"

"No! No!" I protested. I tried every way I could think of to get out of it, but nothing worked. It soon became apparent that if they had to drag me back, screaming and kicking, that's exactly what they'd do.

It was spring of 1951; as a going-away present, my boss gave me two weeks' vacation with pay. I wanted to see my family in

New York and asked him if he thought I could fly the plane back there, a distance of about a thousand miles.

I had a student pilot's permit and twenty hours' total flying time—none of it cross-country.

"I don't see why not," he assured me. "You'll do just fine."

Things were more casual then.

The airplane had no radio and no navigational equipment, except for a magnetic compass in the rear cockpit. So I drew a course line on a chart, tucked it under my leg so it wouldn't blow out of the cockpit, and took off.

It took me four hours to reach my first fuel stop near St. Louis, and that part of the trip was uneventful, except for the fact that I learned never to drink a big cup of coffee before embarking on a long flight!

Heading east out of St. Louis, I decided to follow U.S. 40 and dispense with the compass. This allowed me to fly from the airplane's front cockpit, where the airflow was smoother, and I didn't get as much of a draft.

I had decided that my next fuel stop would be at the Waco Airfield in Troy, Ohio. There I thought I would indulge myself in a little nostalgia. I knew the Waco biplanes had been built there—and the Airman's Guide said fuel was available.

From the air, it looked like a beautiful, old-time grass airfield.

But upon landing, I discovered that things aren't always what they seem from the air. The grass wasn't grass at all, it was unmowed hay. And there were no signs of life at the field anywhere—except for the thousands of insects my landing had stirred up!

I took off through the hay, flew to the nearby town of Urbana, gassed up, and headed for Cleveland. It had been my intention to fly over Cleveland, where I could pick up the Lake Erie shore, and then follow that all the way to Ripley.

However, because I had been forced to make an unscheduled stop, I was now running behind schedule. The sun was slowly slipping toward the western horizon, and I was not interested in trying to find Ripley's unlighted airport in the dark. I landed at a suburban Cleveland airport, found an inexpensive motel nearby, and decided that I would get an early start the following morning.

When morning came, the sky looked perfectly clear, so I figured there was no need to call in and get a briefing on the weather. After all, all I had to do was follow the shore of Lake Erie, and that surely shouldn't be too hard.

However, as I climbed, thin wisps of white clouds began flashing past the windshield. For a few moments, the clouds became thicker . . . and then I was sailing along in clear blue skies again.

But when I looked down, my heart took a leap into my throat. The ground was gone.

Beneath me, and in every direction as far as I could see, there was a solid, dazzling white cloud. I had discovered something every pilot learns: The thin stratus layer of cloud, which looks nearly transparent when viewed from below, can sometimes be opaque when viewed from above, with the sun reflecting from its surface.

I flew around aimlessly for a while, looking for a hole through the cloud, but there was none to be found.

I thought of the compass, which I had left back in the rear cockpit. It wasn't going to do me any good back there! I was lost and beginning to feel helpless.

I decided that the only thing to do was descend through the cloud layer, take a look around, and see if I could figure out where I was. I pushed the plane into a very shallow descent. I didn't want to go down too fast, because I had no idea what the terrain beneath me was like.

Going down, I realized that the cloud was getting thicker. It took me longer to get through it going down than it had going up.

When I finally broke through, I didn't like what I saw. I was over a residential area—just where, I had no idea—and I was getting uncomfortably close to the treetops and chimneys below.

I decided to climb back up to think things over. Still, there was cloud cover as far as I could see. After further aimless flying, I realized that the answer was not up there, so I put the plane into another shallow dive. This time I was flying over open country, with no chimneys and not nearly as many trees below.

But there were other problems. This was hilly country, and the hills were getting progressively higher. I had to keep flying up and down, over the tops of the hills, to stay in the clear. And as the hills were getting higher, I would be in the overcast as I crested each hill. The situation did not look good.

I saw another green hill looming just ahead. This would be the last one. I would fly over it, and if there was nothing on the other side, I'd go back above the cloud layer and do some more serious thinking.

I eased up over the hill, with cloud whipping past the windshield. Down the other side of the hill. And there, directly in front of me and just a few hundred feet below, was the most beautiful airport I had ever seen. A mere thirty seconds later, my wheels were on the runway!

That was the day I learned an important lesson: In flying you never assume anything or take anything for granted, and you always have an alternate plan.

I waited most of the day at that little airport for the weather to clear. I discovered that I had landed at Chardon, Ohio, which is several miles east of Cleveland, and that a low stratus layer had moved in rapidly from the lake early that morning.

Since then, I have also become familiar with Chardon as the site of a VOR navigation radio station, which is used in the high-altitude, transcontinental jet route system. In all the years since that day, whenever air traffic control tells me, "You are cleared to Chardon," I feel a warm glow of gratitude for that providential little airport that saved my life back in 1951, and to God for leading me to it even while I was turned away from Him.

The rest of my trip home was uneventful, and I had a much more pleasant flight back to Tulsa.

When I got there, I sold my half of the airplane for two hundred dollars and used that money to buy Patricia an engagement ring and a wedding band. We were married in her church and headed off to the Pacific Northwest to be a military family.

The navy wanted to put me back in the job I had had three years earlier, which was repairing training aids. But I was finally able to convince someone that all the flight training I had received since then could be put to better use, so I was assigned as a flight engineer on a flying boat stationed in northwestern Washington State. Our daughter Debbie was born there, in the small navy hospital on Whidbey Island in Puget Sound.

In 1953, when that tour of duty was up, the flying experience I'd gained aboard that patrol bomber allowed me to obtain a job as a flight engineer with TWA. I would be working on the Constellations, and I was ecstatic. The second stint in the navy may have delayed my dreams for a while, but now everything was back on track.

We relocated to Kansas City, Patricia soon became pregnant again, and things were rosy. In 1955, we even managed to buy a little tract home. While the house was under construction, we drove by to see it at least every other day, holding hands and laughing, walking from room to room, marveling at the fact that we were actually going to be homeowners!

One late December afternoon, we were returning from one of those many trips to our new house. Earlier in the day, we had also spent several hours Christmas shopping, and the car was filled with colorful packages. There were dolls and dresses for Debbie, who was two, and an assortment of toys for our little baby Bill, who was four months old and about to experience his first Christmas.

We were in a happy, holiday mood, bubbling with excitement about the good days just ahead.

Then, suddenly, a car coming the other way swerved directly into our path. I saw him coming, but there was nothing I could do.

I heard Patricia scream, then the first sickening sounds of

metal grinding into metal . . . and then there was silence . . . and darkness.

When I woke up, I was lying in a hospital bed, and I hurt all over—especially my chest and my left foot. As my eyes began to focus, I noticed a nurse looking down at me, with a concerned look on her face. Then it all came back to me—Pat's scream, the helpless frozen feeling of seeing the other car speeding right toward us and not being able to do anything about it.

"Where's my wife?"

"She's okay, Mr. Testrake. She was banged up pretty good—but she'll be fine."

"And my kids? How's Debbie? How's my little boy?"

I could tell from the look on her face that I had asked the wrong question.

"You just relax and try to take it easy. The doctor will be in soon to talk to you. He'll answer all your questions."

I sank back into the bed. If she didn't want to tell me, I knew the news wasn't good. Somehow I knew, even before they told me, that my baby boy was dead.

When the doctor finally came in, he confirmed my fears. Little Bill had been dead at the scene of the accident. Debbie had been injured, but not severely, and she should have no lasting injuries.

I was still reeling from the news of my son's death, but the doctor had more bad news.

"Your foot's in really bad shape," he told me. "We've tried, but there's nothing we can do. We're going to have to amputate."

Before I could even absorb this latest bit of news, he told me that the surgery had already been scheduled.

Meanwhile, my boss, Chief Flight Engineer Al Brick, had happened to hear of the accident on the ten o'clock news. He didn't know me personally, but when he heard my name, he realized that I was one of his aviators.

He immediately checked into the situation and found out where I was and what my condition was. Then he called my mother back in Ripley and made arrangements to fly her to Kansas City the next day.

She would be coming on a feeder airline out of Erie, Pennsylvania, and connecting with a TWA flight in Pittsburgh. I discovered later that her flight coming out of Erie was an hour late arriving in Pittsburgh, but in order to get her to Kansas City as quickly as possible, TWA held up their flight in Pittsburgh just to wait for her.

The TWA airliner sat at the gate, fueled up, full of passengers, and all ready to go—waiting for my mother so she could be brought to the bedside of her injured son.

She arrived at the hospital just as I was about to be wheeled into surgery to have my foot amputated.

As soon as she got there, she called a halt to the proceedings. The doctors argued with her, of course, but Mom was adamant, and they were unable to convince her that my foot had to be removed.

Once she had delayed the surgery, she went about the task of finding out the name of the best bone surgeon in Kansas City. And when she had found him, she had me transferred to his hospital and engaged his services to save my foot.

And that's what he did. He completely rebuilt my foot using plastic bones. Today, more than thirty years later, when I'm walking up and down the sixty acres of my farm, I gratefully remember the man who saved my foot when everyone else was saying it couldn't be done.

But what I really needed at the time was not so much someone to rebuild my foot as it was someone to rebuild my life.

I was no stranger to tragedy. My father had died several years before, at a very young age, but this new sorrow was more than I could bear. How could I ever deal with the loss of our beautiful little baby boy? Just four months earlier we had been so happy when he came into our lives, and now he was gone. Gone before we ever really got a chance to know him—a happy, smiling, good-natured baby killed by a drunk driver who couldn't keep his car on the right side of the highway.

And what about the other driver and his passenger? They had both died in the accident, too. How could there be reason and meaning in a world where such terrible things could happen?

One day, shortly after the accident, a man came to see me. He was a flight engineer with TWA and had been with the airline for a number of years. His name was Barney Garriott.

My mind was reeling and confused, so I don't remember a great deal about his early visit. But I do remember that he told me God was with me. And for some reason, at a time when I had been doubting the very existence of God, I believed him. When Barney told me that God was there in that hospital room with me, I felt a warm, glowing sensation, starting in my chest and spreading throughout my entire body. There was no intellectual reason for that experience, but it happened, and it convinced me that my newfound friend was telling the truth. There was also something about his manner—his quiet confidence and strength—that made me believe what he said.

During the next three weeks, while I remained in the hospital, Barney came to see me almost every day. I was amazed that a man who had been a stranger to me before should now seem to care so much, but it was obvious that he did care.

One day he came into the room carrying a little book.

He sat down, pulled a chair up close to my bedside, and gave me his mischievous wink.

"How you doing today, John?"

"Not too bad," I answered. I was always glad to see him; I just seemed to feel better when he came for a visit.

"Brought something for you to read today."

"Great."

"It's a little book called *Peace With God*. I'm going to leave it with you . . . but I want you to promise me you'll read it."

Because it seemed so important to him, I promised. He had

been good to me, and if it would make him happy, that was fine with me.

It turned out that the little book, written by Billy Graham, was a basic introduction to Christianity. It was straightforward and simple, but much of it was new to me. I am sure I had heard similar messages before, but they had never really registered.

At first, I didn't have much interest in the book—it wasn't as exciting as those adventure novels I had loved so much as a kid. But Barney wasn't going to let me get by without reading it. He came back every day, and he'd always quiz me.

"Are you reading the book?" he'd ask. "How far are you?" "What did you think about the part where he says . . . ?" "Do you have any questions?"

I had no choice but to keep reading. And before long, I was thoroughly enjoying it and thinking a lot about some of the things Dr. Graham had to say. I was becoming more and more convinced that Jesus Christ really was the Son of God, and that He had died so that I might have forgiveness of my sins.

Finally, the day came when I finished the book. Right on schedule, my friend came to see me.

"Well?" he asked me, when I told him I had finished the book.

"Well what?"

"What do you think?"

"About what?" I guess I knew what he was getting at but wasn't ready to admit it.

"Don't you think maybe you ought to give your life to Christ?"

For some reason, the question made me angry and defensive.

"Well, now hold on here," I bristled. "That's a pretty serious thing, and I don't want to rush into anything like that. Maybe I ought to think about it some more!"

"Okay, John. You do that."

I was surprised that he gave up so easily, but he didn't push, and we enjoyed the rest of his visit talking about the weather, or flying, or something equally as innocuous.

Finally, I was able to go home from the hospital, but I was still confined to a wheelchair. Barney would come by often to talk and to see if Patricia and I needed anything.

Then, one night he literally backed me into the corner of my kitchen. I was in my wheelchair, and he got a kitchen chair and set it down about a foot in front of me, and he went back over the entire matter.

There was none of the usual sparkle in his eyes, only a stern seriousness.

"You do believe in God?" he asked me.

"Yes."

"And you do believe in Jesus?"

I swallowed. "Yes."

"And you do believe that God sent Jesus to take care of your sins for you?"

I realized now that I did believe that, too.

"Yes."

"Well, then," he pushed on, "there's no reason for you not to accept Him, is there?"

I knew he had me. There was nothing else for me to do. So I took a deep breath, gulped, and stammered out a weak, "Yes."

"Yes what?"

"Yes, I accept Jesus Christ as my Lord and Savior!"

As soon as those words had come out of my mouth, I felt as if I were going to bump my head on the ceiling. When people talk about being on cloud nine, I always remember that experience, because it was as if I was floating away on a cloud of absolute bliss and total joy.

Patricia, of course, was delighted that I had accepted the Lord, for she had always been close to the Lord, and her own faith had sustained her during the time of our loss.

We began attending church together, and I became truly concerned about trying to live for the Lord. For the first time, my life had a real meaning. I knew why I had been born and understood that in every situation my calling was to serve God and give Him glory.

I still didn't understand why little Bill had to die, and I missed him terribly. I knew that Patricia felt the pain even more deeply, because a little baby is so totally dependent upon his mother. But we were helped immensely by Leslie Weatherhead's "The Will of God," which spoke of the difference between God's perfect will and His permissive will. The pamphlet helped me to realize that it wasn't God's will that our baby should die at the hands of a drunk. But God, in His mercy and wisdom, had taken this terrible thing and brought something very good out of it!

I knew, too, that our little baby had gone home, to be with His Creator, and that someday we would be reunited with him.

Very soon, we were rejoicing over the news that Patricia was pregnant again. This time, another little boy became part of our family, and we named him Alan. Alan was followed shortly by another daughter, Diane. And before too long, we were too busy raising our children and rejoicing in the Lord to dwell on the tragedy that had taken our son from us.

3

At Home on the Farm

The next few years were peaceful ones, and it seemed that life would roll by in an unending stream of "happily ever after." Patricia and I were happy with our marriage, our children, and our relationship with God.

Of course, the "happily ever after" part was not to be—at least not just yet. There were other tragedies waiting down the road—but at that point, everything was fine.

In the late fifties, Pat's parents came to live with us. Her father, a building contractor, had a bleeding ulcer that forced him to retire, so they came to Kansas City from Tulsa. Our little tract home, the one we had been so very proud of just a few years before, was suddenly much too tiny. As I looked around our Kansas City neighborhood, I also realized that this was not the best place in the world to raise children.

Our children were still small. Debbie was ready to start first grade, and the other two were younger—but I worried about what life would be like for them in the city when they got older. Some of our neighbors had had problems with their teenaged children—problems that I thought were brought about largely by the city environment, so I called a family meeting to talk about what we should do.

We had a long, round-table discussion, at which it was decided we would put the house up for sale and look for a farm.

I got a map of the area and drew a circle around Kansas City Municipal Airport with a radius of fifty miles. I felt that was the maximum distance I cared to drive to work.

That spring and summer, my father-in-law and I spent all of our spare time driving around looking for farmland, but we could find nothing that suited our purposes.

By late summer, we had worked our way to the little town of Richmond, which is about fifty miles northeast of Kansas City. I had never been in Richmond before and probably hadn't even known the town existed before I began my search for a farm. But there was a real estate office there, and, yes, the man knew of a nice farm for sale.

What we saw when we got there was sixty acres of gently rolling hills, on which sat a two-bedroom house, shaded by an enormous elm tree and overlooking the broad Missouri River Valley. We discovered there was an abundant supply of spring water, and the taxes were low. This was the best place we had seen—and even if it hadn't been so great, we were getting mighty tired of looking. So, for fifteen thousand dollars we bought the property and began cleaning up and fixing up.

Late that year of 1959 we moved into our new farmhouse. We were much more crowded here than we had been in our little tract home, but at least there was room for growth—a lot of growth!

The first winter in the house was a rough one. The grandparents used one bedroom, and the three children used the other.

Pat and I slept out on what was a closed-in porch, but it hadn't been closed in all that well. The windows seemed to be an afterthought, and they let the snow and cold wind blow in freely. Many mornings we would awaken to find an additional blanket of snow spread evenly over our bed. But I guess it was healthy— we didn't catch one cold that winter.

We went right to work fixing the place up—adding on and spreading out—until we had room for everyone. The first priority was building a small house in the adjacent pasture for our parents, followed by a barn constructed of native Missouri oak. The barn was painted red with a white trim, to reflect my Yankee heritage. I already knew how to do electrical work, my father-in-law taught me carpentry and masonry, and we learned plumbing together—with septic tanks ordered from the Sears catalog.

Our house was next, and it's been added to and improved upon in the quarter-century since.

In 1962, our son Johnny was born here. His birth added to our happiness and joy in the Lord.

Over the years, the farm has seen many changes. We raised cattle, sold hay, raised horses, and now we're growing grapes just as my grandfather and my father did in New York.

But since 1959, this farm has been my home . . . and it was the place I longed to see most during my forced stay in Beirut.

Meanwhile, I was moving up the ladder at TWA. I had begun as a flight engineer, but along the way my astigmatism suddenly disappeared, and my vision became perfect at twenty-twenty. I was then able to become a first officer (something that would not have been possible at American Airlines), and I had later earned my captain's wings.

Obtaining those wings was not easy, and every time I look at them I am reminded once again of God's loving care and guidance, and how He rescues us just when we've come to the end of ourselves and have no choice but to turn things over to Him.

Being a successful airline pilot depends largely on having a positive frame of mind. If you think you can do it, then you probably can, but if you're afraid you can't do it, then chances are you can't. It's a take-charge position, and it's common knowledge that nearly every airline captain thinks he is the best one in the business. That sort of self-confidence is a necessary ingredient in the makeup of the successful pilot.

One reason for that is that the pilot has tremendous responsibilities riding on his shoulders. It's totally up to the pilot, for instance, to decide when weather conditions might not be safe for flying, and he has to trust himself and know that his judgment is good. Is it too stormy to fly? What about the icy conditions? Unless the airport is completely closed down, those judgments are left entirely up to the pilot.

All the pilots I know would rather err on the side of caution. They don't want to take any unnecessary risks, and that's the way the airlines train them to be.

Many people think that once the plane is in the air, the pilot is in the hands of air traffic controllers, but that's only partly true. If the pilot disagrees on grounds of safety with an instruction he has been given by the controller, he is free to reject it and request an alternate plan. The safety of his passengers always comes first for the professional airline pilot.

As long as I'm on the subject of safety, I ought to say that there isn't a single airport in the United States that I dislike flying into or out of because I don't think it's safe. I've seen news stories saying that some airports are "accidents waiting to happen," but I personally believe that's the news media at its sensation-seeking worst, looking for some headlines to sell newspapers. There are several airports, such as Washington National, which are used to full capacity, but the Federal Aviation Administration won't allow them to go beyond a reasonable level.

The FAA keeps tight control on the number of flights an airport can handle each day. That's why you hear of some airlines that would like to have, say, eight or nine flights into an airport, but the FAA will allow only five or six.

It's frustrating sometimes to be sitting in the airplane for half an hour or so waiting for clearance to take off, but that too is a matter of safety. No more traffic is allowed than the air traffic controllers can safely handle. Sitting at the end of the runway is inconvenient, and it wastes fuel, but it's not dangerous.

When my turn came to move into the captain's seat, I'd been a copilot for about six years, and during that time I had come to think that I was very good at what I did. I had the confidence that would allow me to do a good job as captain. But the problem was that I was really borrowing on the captain's expertise and thinking it was my own. After all, the captain was the fellow sitting up there in the left front seat, and if something went wrong he had the primary responsibility of remedying the situation.

My job as the copilot was to carry out the captain's orders, which came in many ways, depending upon his personality. Sometimes there would be direct orders and at other times gentle hints.

But whatever the case, things got done the way the captain wanted, and as the copilot I would say, "Yes, sir," and do it his way.

After a while, though, I began to think that I was the one doing all this expert maneuvering and bringing the ship safely through the dark, the wind, and the storm.

So when the time came for my promotion to captain, I was sure I was ready. But I discovered, about midway through the upgrading program, that I wasn't quite as smart as I had been thinking I was. Because now, instead of having the captain sitting beside me telling me what to do, *I* was in the captain's seat. And there beside me was a check-pilot, looking over my shoulder and taking notes on everything I did. I knew that it was not the check-pilot's duty to immediately call my attention to or correct any mistakes I made. Instead, if I made one wrong maneuver, his job was to allow me to go on down the wrong road until my error became obvious to everyone, or until he finally had to step in to rectify the situation.

Three or four times during the upgrading period I made blunders and did things I knew I wasn't supposed to do. But I always dismissed them as momentary aberrations and felt that I was doing okay overall.

Then one day I was called into the office and told that I would be going for an evaluation ride with another check-captain. I knew what this meant: My check-captain was not convinced I had what it takes to be a captain. I was being given a one-shot, make-it-or-break-it deal. My entire career was hanging on how well I did on this one trip.

If this pilot agreed with the first check-captain's assessment of my abilities, my upgrading would be refused. And at that time, the airline's policy was that if you flunked upgrading you were fired. I would be out on the street looking for another job.

I had worked in the training department as a flight engineer flight instructor, so I knew exactly what the score was, and it shook me to my very foundations.

As if I wasn't already worried enough, they assigned as my check-captain a pilot who had a reputation of being hard-nosed and tough. He wasn't the sort of man to give breaks or look the other way at even the simplest mistakes.

I went and talked to my minister and told him, "I'm going out on a one-shot ride, and I don't know what's going to happen, but I could very well wind up unemployed." All of the confidence I had built up during my years of service with the airline had vanished into the blue sky.

But after talking with the minister and praying about it, I received a sense of assurance and peace. My confidence began to come back, and I knew, somehow, that the trip was going to go well. And it did. I sailed through it without the slightest hitch.

"I don't see anything wrong with you at all," the check-pilot told me when the trip was over. "I'm going to set you up for a semifinal check-ride."

One hurdle down, one more to go. Now I was up to where I would have been had I not made those mistakes in the beginning.

And everyone knew that the semifinal check-ride was the most important ride of all. If you did okay on that, the final ride was really not much more than a formality. Those who breezed through the semifinal were sure to receive their upgrading to captain.

Finally, the big day came. Once again I was faced with a make-it-or-break-it opportunity. The check-pilot was a friend of mine, a man I knew to be fair but tough. He wouldn't make it easy on me, but he wouldn't make it any harder than was necessary to insure that I would be a capable, dependable pilot.

For some reason, as we were walking out to the aircraft I began to feel slightly uneasy and nervous. I tried to shake it off, but I couldn't. Meanwhile, my friend was giving me his usual pep talk.

"There's no big deal about this," he said. "All you have to do is just go out and fly the airplane from A to B like you would any other time. And if you do, then you get signed off."

When we reached the cockpit, I settled into the captain's chair, while he buckled himself into the copilot's seat. An inspector from the Federal Aviation Administration was also going along on the first leg of the flight.

The preflight check went fine, and I kept telling myself that there was no basis for my uneasiness. I knew everything I needed to know, I felt comfortable in this cockpit, and I had flown the route many times as a copilot.

"This ought to be a piece of cake," I told myself.

The first leg of the flight took us from Kansas City into Chicago, and as we were heading into O'Hare, the controller did something that caught me completely by surprise. I had been flying in and out of Chicago for years, and I thought I knew exactly how they did things. But on this occasion, the controller brought me in close to the airport at a high altitude and then cleared me for a visual approach. I wasn't used to that and didn't expect it, so I didn't respond as rapidly or as aggressively as I should have.

I wound up making what I considered to be a "ratty" approach. Had I jumped right on it when the controller cleared me for a visual approach, I would have been fine, but I had hesitated, and that's one thing a pilot cannot afford to do.

You learn very quickly in aviation that the pilot must stay ahead of the airplane at all times. You must anticipate and react quickly. If you let the airplane get ahead of you, to the point where you're following it instead of the other way around, you can find yourself in deep trouble. And, for a few minutes, that's what I had done. There was nothing dangerous about the landing, but it wasn't picture perfect, and it was met with deafening silence by the other men in the cockpit. They didn't say anything bad about it, but their silence said plenty to me.

The FAA man got off in Chicago, while the rest of us headed for New York and JFK.

As we made our approach to New York, the controller told me that we'd be making the Canarsie approach, which is a twisting, complicated pattern, with several altitude changes. I don't know if that's what did it, but suddenly I felt as if a heavy weight had been placed on my shoulders. I had a jet airliner full of passengers who were counting on me. Was I worthy of their confidence? Who was I to think I could be responsible for all these people?

I knew it was up to me to get them safely on the ground, and I thought, *What on earth are you doing here? What business do you have thinking you're an airline captain?*

There was really no reason for any of those thoughts. I had been flying for years without a mishap, and I was perfectly capable of dealing with any situation that arose. Still, whatever self-confidence I had simply vanished. I had never felt so unsure of myself.

I went ahead and made the approach, and even though there was nothing really wrong with it, I knew my confidence had been shaken. I only hoped that the check-pilot couldn't see how nervous I was. By the time we walked into the office at Kennedy my knees were beginning to wobble.

We were on the ground at Kennedy for a few minutes, and then it was on to Indianapolis. It was dark by the time we got there, and I was still feeling rattled from the sloppy approach I had made at O'Hare and the blows my self-confidence had taken at Kennedy.

It was a beautiful, starlit night, and the lights of Indianapolis were clearly visible below as we began our descent into the city. The approach was straight in, with nothing complicated or difficult about it. But my brain was beginning to lock up on me. I blew a very simple turn, overshot the final approach course, and had to turn around on the other side and fishtail back. It was a very amateurish approach and I was ashamed of myself. There wasn't anything dangerous about it, but it just wasn't a professional job, and I knew the check-pilot was aware that I was not keeping on top of things.

Not a word was said as we taxied to our gate. What could be said? Both of us knew I hadn't done well, and there was no sense in talking about it. But still, the silence was distressing, and I began to feel as if I was drowning in a sea of depression. A deep, dark feeling descended over me. I was choking under pressure, failing just when I needed most to succeed.

We had one more leg to fly that night, to Cleveland. There was nothing to do but press on, even though I felt as if my career had already literally flown away.

As I got back into the captain's seat after picking up the weather and other information at Indianapolis, it occurred to me to give my worries to the Lord. I bowed my head, closed my eyes, and silently prayed, "Lord, I am at the end of my rope. I can't do this alone. If You want me to be an airline pilot, then You're going to have to pull it out of the fire."

Not more than fifteen seconds after I'd said that prayer, I felt the weight just lift from me. It disappeared totally, and I felt light and free. I even felt exhilarated and confident, in spite of the

45

fact that my trip had been anything but successful up to that point.

I realized, too, that if God wanted me to be an airline pilot, I would be one. If He didn't, I had no chance of ever becoming one anyway. And I knew that whatever He wanted was best for me. How good it felt to rest in His will.

I didn't actually grin, but I wanted to. I knew the trip to Cleveland would be a good one. And it was. I had never flown a better flight in my life. I was on top of things the entire way, kept ahead of the airplane, had all the checkpoints down pat, flew the approach perfectly, and everything went the way it was supposed to. Most important, I felt good—in charge of the situation.

I suppose by that time my check-pilot was going through some inner turmoil. He was a friend of mine, someone I had known for years, and he didn't want to fire me. Yet it was his job to see to it that only the most qualified made it to the rank of captain. I think he had just about made up his mind to give me the boot, because I had been acting uncertain and hesitant.

He had seen a good flight on that last leg of the trip, but that was only one good one against three not-so-good ones.

The next morning, we met in the coffee shop for breakfast. There were the two of us, along with the flight engineer and three flight attendants, and I was the life of the party, cracking jokes and acting supremely confident. The check-pilot sat across from me, taking it all in, and I'm sure he wondered what was going on. For most of the day before I had been the epitome of self-doubt, and here I was carrying on as if I didn't have a care in the world, acting like an experienced, hard-charging airline captain. He didn't understand that the Lord had made the difference in me— and I didn't understand that I had been chastised and disciplined by the Master Teacher.

We had to fly two legs that day—from Cleveland to St. Louis and then on to Kansas City—and both were a repeat of the night before. It all clicked into place, everything went exactly the way it was supposed to, and there was no way the check-pilot could criticize anything I had done.

When the trip was over, we landed in Kansas City, and I shut down the engines.

We sat there for a few minutes, while I waited for the check-pilot's reaction. The flight engineer finished with his business, said good-bye, and left the cockpit, and still nothing was said.

Finally, he said, "Well, I'm going to pass you. I just want to tell you this. Better keep your head out of the cockpit, especially when you're flying around places like O'Hare. There's a lot of stuff you can run into up there. You get your nose buried inside the cockpit, and you'll be in big trouble."

I said, "Yes, sir!" And, I thought, *I'll take any chewing out you want to give me, just as long as you pass me.*

I felt I had passed more than a test to become an airline pilot. I had learned a valuable lesson in trusting God, and in bringing my will into agreement with His. That lesson would serve me very well during my career as a pilot, and it's something I have never forgotten.

Over the years, my family had become well-settled into the life of an airline flight engineer, copilot, and now pilot. It was and is an ideal way of life, as far as I'm concerned. I love flying, and I know I could never be happy working a regular job, carrying a briefcase to the office from nine to five every day.

There are few things about the pilot's life that I don't enjoy. Sometimes it's rough being away from home for days at a time, but that's compensated for by the fact that you also get to stay home for days at a time between trips, so it all evens out. Airline pilots are able to spend time with their families that other working men don't get. I have had ample time to work around my farm, tend to my vineyard, and so on. An airline captain does not live the way some people seem to think he does. He is not like an officer in the navy, who may be gone from home for weeks or even months at a time while his wife sits at home and waits for his return.

In fact, if space permits, the pilot's wife can fly with him. It's a great way to see the world, and that's something I have used to the fullest advantage.

I can recall times when being away from home necessitated changes in family life, but as long as the pilot and his family are willing to adjust, everything will work out fine. Once, when the children were small, we had Christmas on January 7, because that was the closest to Christmas I was home. It may have been hard on the children to wait an extra thirteen days to open their presents, but they accepted it with good grace. After all, my schedule was something they'd grown up with, and they understood the way things were. And anyway, when "Christmas" finally did come they thought it was neat to be having an exciting time when the big day was long since over for their friends.

Another time, we were planning a short trip to Miami, but it was dependent upon there being room aboard a flight to Florida. When there wasn't room, we had to make a fast change of plans and wound up in San Francisco instead. But such uncertainty can make life fun and exciting.

When I first went to work for the airlines my older daughter, Debbie, was just a baby, and we had just moved in across the street from Pat's parents in Tulsa. Pat thought she was in heaven because she had her own little house right across the street from her mother, she had her little baby to take care of, and I was going off to work every day carrying my lunch bucket and coming home every night for supper. She was delighted with the life we were living and wanted it to go on forever.

When I suddenly announced that I wanted to go off and take a flying job with TWA in Kansas City, she was crushed. There was an awful uproar. It was so bad that I finally said to her, "If you think it's going to be so bad, here's what I'll do.

"We'll try it for five years, and if at the end of that time you still don't like it, I'll quit and go back to work in the shops—I'll get a ground job."

I suppose that was a take-it-or-leave-it offer, because I was determined that I wanted to at least give flying a try.

So we went off to Kansas City. At the end of five years with TWA, I reminded her of our agreement and asked her what she thought about my giving up my flying job.

She threw back her head and laughed uproariously at the very thought. How could we even consider giving up this way of life? We were both convinced that there couldn't be a better one.

Looking back over the years, I could see the way God had directed my life. I thought about my flight home to Ripley so long ago, and how the little airport appeared just when I was ready to give up. I remembered how I had fought with all my might against going back into the navy during the Korean war—how I wanted so much to take that job offer with American Airlines. But God knew best. I felt that I owed Him so much! My family, my farm, my position with TWA.

I could feel the Lord's blessing on my life, because He was allowing me to do something I loved. And very few people are able to have a career that fulfills their dreams and brings them satisfaction the way mine did (and does) to me.

I resolved that I would try never to question God or fight against His will for my life. I figured that whatever happened, as long as I was trying to serve Him, He would work it out for good. He was in control of everything, and that was all anyone could ask.

Then, sometime in the late sixties, Pat began complaining about not feeling well. She was uncomfortable, actually in quite a bit of pain.

At first, her doctors thought it was due to a bad fall she had taken. She had twisted and sprained her back and had a difficult time bouncing back.

When she complained, doctors assured her that all she needed was time. The pain wasn't going to go away overnight.

But when the pain persisted beyond a reasonable length of time, they began to look for other problems. A cyst was found—a large benign growth. They thought that was the problem, so she underwent surgery. But still, there was no relief from the discomfort.

More tests were ordered, and that's when the terrible verdict came: cancer.

We were both stunned and dazed, and we both cried. How could this happen to us? Life was so good; we had so much going for us. How could this demonic disease get its tentacles on my wife—a loving, caring woman who had been God's greatest gift to me?

We had dozens of questions to ask, which we did, hoping for an encouraging answer. But the answers always seemed doubtful and discouraging.

Pat's cancer had begun in her rectum. If it had been discovered in time, her chances for recovery would have been much better. But the other problems with her back and her benign cyst had masked the real source of her trouble. By the time the cancer was discovered it had metastasized to her brain. To be sure, there was treatment available, but the doctors weren't kidding either one of us about her chances. They were not good.

If only she had never fallen and hurt her back. If only the doctors had looked harder. *If only . . . if only . . . if only.* Thoughts about what might have, could have, should have happened haunted me.

I think Pat accepted the news of her illness much better than I did. After the initial shock, she seemed to face the disease with a calmness. Her faith in God never wavered. Whatever He wanted to do in her life, she would accept it.

She accepted the brain surgery and the long, painful recuperation. She accepted the chemotherapy, which sometimes seemed worse than the disease. She was a wonderful example of grace, faith, and courage. I know she had her moments of doubt and despair. Who wouldn't? But as she grew weaker, and the treatments didn't seem to be killing the cancer, her major concern seemed to be for me and the children. She worried about us and prayed for us and hoped that we would be able to pick up and go on without her, if that was what we had to do.

As for me, I couldn't bear the thought of going on without her, and I told myself over and over again that it wasn't going to happen. Surely God was going to step into our lives with a miracle.

One of these days I would walk into the hospital to visit her, and she'd be sitting up in bed smiling and tell me that something had happened, that she was fine and wanted to go home.

I had sincerely given her over to God's care and keeping. But having prayed the prayer of relinquishment, I was looking confidently for His healing hand. I realize now I was unconsciously playing games. I was saying, "Your will be done." But I was expecting, "My will be done."

I was always looking for something to hold on to. I'd tell myself, *She looks better today. Maybe the treatments are finally starting to work!*

After a while, I think I developed somewhat of a split personality with regards to Pat and her illness. My mind came to understand that she was dying, but my heart was telling me that it just couldn't happen. I think the Lord was anesthetizing me from the pain.

When I went to see her I would talk about bringing her home and tell her what we were going to do when that happened. I'd ramble on about my plans for our future together—but it was a future that was never to be.

On Valentine's Day, 1976, Pat's battle with cancer ended, and she was taken home to be with God. On that day, she was reunited with the baby son we had lost so many years before.

Ever since we had moved to Richmond, Pat and I had been attending a church there. It wasn't the most dynamic or on-fire church in the world, but it had become our church home. We had both been active members and had many good friends there.

When Sunday came, a few days after Pat's death, I knew I wanted and needed to be in the house of God. At this time in my life I needed Him more than I had ever needed Him before. And I think that if I could have thrown my arms around His legs and held on to Him, I would have.

So I went to church, sat way in the back, and sensed that God was there with me. But I noticed something else, too. The other people there did not know how to relate to me or what to say to me, so I was left alone. As I left the church building that Sunday morning, I realized that few of us in that church were really walking closely with the Lord.

We were believers, yes, but most of us had become rather stagnant in our Christian lives, rather than constantly growing closer to God.

Our spiritual lives were largely involved with programs, activities, form, and ritual. We were not challenged to maintain Scripture study. My own Bibles had grown dusty on the shelves.

We didn't really know how to share one another's burdens, as the Scriptures commanded us to do, and each of us tended to deal with his or her own family problems and tragedies privately. I wasn't bitter, or blaming anyone for their lack of support, because I knew if it had been one of them instead of me, I wouldn't know what to do or say either.

But I resolved that day that I was going to get as close to the Lord as I could. I really wanted to know Him and love Him in a way I never had before.

So in the days and weeks following Patricia's death I really tried to spend time with Him: reading the Bible, praying, and just waiting on Him.

I don't mean to imply that He made coping with Pat's death easy. I cried often, and I'm sure the kids did, too. Yet the Lord was there with me, sustaining me, and I came to sense His presence in a new way.

I comforted myself, too, with the fact that I had spent twenty-three years with the finest Christian woman I could ever have hoped to find, and that was much more than many men got. I had enough happy memories to last me for the rest of my life—and when that life was over, I'd be able to see her again!

I decided that my priority should be to finish raising my children. I would help them get through school, see that they were well established in their chosen professions, and then I would decide what to do with the rest of my life.

I think Pat's death hit our two youngest children the hardest. Diane was a senior in high school, a young woman just ready to step out into the world. She needed her mother's loving guidance and inspiration. Johnny was just thirteen, passing through the most difficult years of life, and if anyone needed his mother's strong Christian influence, he did.

After Diane graduated, I thought that if she went away to college it would help to get her mind off her loss and help her through the tough times. But I was wrong.

The other girls in the dorm had mothers who called them every day on the telephone, who laughed and cried with them, gave them motherly advice, and listened when they needed a shoulder to cry on. They had mothers who sent them care packages, sewed lacy curtains for the dorm windows, and did all the other loving things that mothers do.

But there was Diane, all by herself, with nobody to look after her except her father, who didn't think about those sorts of things. So college life only intensified Diane's loneliness and sense of loss. She made it through the first year, but then decided she'd had enough and dropped out.

It was hard for me to give my children all the love and attention they needed, because I was lonely and empty myself. The Lord was there, but I needed someone I could put my arms around and hold close.

In the late fall, several months after Pat's death, I went back to New York to visit my mother.

While I was there, she asked me if I had considered trying to meet any other women.

"No, Mom," I told her. "I'm not really interested."

"Well, I really think you should consider it."

"Oh, Mom . . . ," I sighed. "I don't think I'm ready for that. Besides, you know I could never find anyone to replace Pat."

But she was persistent: "I just think you need somebody. You're still a young man, and there's no reason why you should spend the rest of your life alone."

Then, on the flight back to Kansas City, I was sitting with a friend, who is also a pilot for TWA, and he mentioned how nice the flight attendant who was serving our part of the cabin seemed to be.

He was right . . . she was friendly.

He mentioned that she had a terrific personality.

Right again.

And had I noticed how attractive she was?

Yes, as a matter of fact, I had noticed.

"You know," he said, "she's a widow." It seemed that her husband had died in an accident some time before, he told me, and it was probably about time for her to think about dating again.

"Maybe you should give her a call," he said.

"No . . . I don't think so."

But my mother had planted the seed, and my friend was watering it. I was tired of being alone. Maybe it *was* time I started dating. The more I watched this young woman, the more I liked what I saw. I finally decided that when we got to Kansas City I would go up and ask her for a date.

It wouldn't be easy. I hadn't asked anyone for a date in nearly twenty-five years and wasn't sure I could remember how! But I'd try.

But the closer we got to Kansas City, the more it seemed that I was rushing things—so I thanked her for helping us have a pleasant trip, and that was all. I'm not sure now whether I was chickening out . . . but that might have had something to do with it. Then again, perhaps it had something to do with the Lord, His timing, and the person *He* had in mind for me!

Back in Richmond, just a day or two later, I was in the hardware store, looking for some tools I needed for my work on the farm. When I got to the checkout counter there was a strikingly beautiful woman paying for her purchases.

I knew the woman working the cash register, so I said, "Aren't you going to introduce me to your friend here?" I wasn't going to let this one get away without at least an introduction.

After the introduction, she picked up her package and walked out of the store. I turned to the clerk and asked, "Who in the world was that?"

I then grilled her for the next five or ten minutes, finding out everything she knew about this lovely creature.

Besides her name, I learned that she was a divorcée and, even better than that, I found out where she lived.

I also found my courage. I went directly to her house, struck up a conversation, and asked her for a date.

It didn't take too many dates before she had swept me off my feet. I was in love and thinking of marriage, and there was no doubt in my mind that she was thinking along the same lines. We just had such a good time when we were together!

Judy was raising two daughters alone and doing a good job of it, but facing the usual problems of single parents. Money was not plentiful and she denied herself in order to provide for her children. I also felt that her business associates were not giving her a fair shake.

The net effect of all of this was that it made me fiercely protective. She seemed to me to be a damsel in distress, and I decided that I was her knight in shining armor. She needed someone to take care of her and shield her from all of life's troubles. And who better than me?

I went to the jewelry store, picked out a large, expensive diamond ring, and at Christmas that year, I asked her to marry me.

She accepted the diamond ring with grace and charm, and yet I could see that it came as a surprise. She hadn't been expecting anything like this and didn't know what to do.

We were approaching the idea of marriage from two totally different angles: I had had a good marriage and wanted to bring it back. She had had bad luck and was afraid of getting burned again.

She was having fun with the romance of the situation. She enjoyed talking about where we were going to go on our honeymoon and things like that.

But whenever I started talking about the wedding itself, her reaction was always, "Oh, let's not pin it down to a certain day yet." She was always elusive when it came to specifics.

She was much wiser than I and soon saw that our personalities were not matched for marriage. She broke off our engagement, and by the end of January, our relationship had come to an end. Whatever we had was gone, and, try as I might, I could not bring it back.

When our relationship ended, I was despondent and angry, and I told the Lord how I felt.

"It's not fair!" I cried out. "I lost my first true love just a year ago, and now when I find someone else, I lose her, too!"

I wanted Him to tell me what was going on, but He didn't say anything. He just let me lie there, wallowing in self-pity, spending sleepless nights staring at the ceiling, until the day came when I finally gave up, trusted Him, and accepted the situation with good grace and a smile.

Then, the following Sunday morning in February, I walked into church and saw an attractive woman I had never seen before talking to one of my friends.

I walked up to them and tapped him on the shoulder.

"Who is this young lady you're not introducing me to?"

I recognized her name when he told me. Phyllis was a schoolteacher who had recently been divorced. She had three children, and she was a member of my church—even though I had never met her before.

It seems strange to me that in a town of only five thousand people, Phyllis and I had lived within shouting distance for several years and had never met or spoken to each other, yet, that was the way it was. When I walked into church on that Sunday morning and saw her there, I knew immediately that there was something very special about her.

By that night I had a date with her and three days later another. And then many more in rapid succession.

Having so recently been burned, I was wary of another serious attachment so soon. Yet, I couldn't help myself because it felt so good to be with her, and we seemed to enjoy each other's company no matter what we were doing. It is as if God tapped me on the shoulder that day in church and said, "This is the one for you, John."

We were married in our church on June 19, 1977, and Phyllis asked one of her friends to sing "Evergreen" at our wedding. It was a good choice.

I could only get four days for our honeymoon between my trips, so we opted for a quick trip to San Francisco, and I introduced my bride to one of my favorite cities. We dined in rooftop restaurants with the fog swirling outside, laughed like kids on the cable cars, ate shrimp at the wharf, and shivered and hugged on the bay cruise boats.

After our return home, we set up housekeeping at the farm and undertook the sometimes-frustrating, always-challenging task of merging two families of children. Of my children, Debbie was well launched on her career as a registered nurse, Alan was in college, Diane soon left for marriage and her own family, and so John B. was left with us to finish high school. We fixed up a bachelor apartment in the basement for him so he could be the suave gent and entertain his friends in style. We told people that he lived under the house.

Of Phyllis's three children, Russ was away in the Marine Corps, Jeff came and went with the rise and fall of his fortunes, and Cindy stayed with us to finish high school. We gave her Debbie's old room, and, though their occupancy was separated by several years, it had the same effect on both girls: long hours engaged in mysterious female rites with the door closed; the only sign of life, the bad music coming from within; and a strong reluctance to come out for furniture dusting or supper preparation.

Diane had an especially difficult situation to deal with. Still sorely missing her mother, she had found solace and healing in returning home and taking up housekeeping for her dad and brother, only to be almost immediately displaced as mistress of the house by another woman. She had been very supportive during my courtship and had given much good advice to the rusty suitor. But this was a cruel twist that none of us had foreseen. Her solution was to leave. She was angry and with reason, but since she's as good-hearted as her mother was, that did not last. She now lives close by with her husband and three sons, and we are good friends.

Cindy's situation was different, but equally difficult to cope with.

When her parents had split up, Cindy had hung on to the hope that it was only temporary, and that they would get back together. She saw me as an intruder who was ruining the chance of that happening, and she resented me for it.

She would do little things to let me know how she felt, and that was a difficult time for me, because I wanted to love her and have her love me, too. I wanted her to understand that I loved and cared for her mother, and that I had had nothing to do with the fact that her parents just could not make a go of their marriage.

Some mornings, Phyllis and I would be sitting at the breakfast table when Cindy left for school. She would stick her head into the dining room and call our cheerily, "Bye, Mom!" She was ignoring me and it hurt. But I understood how she felt, and I hurt for her, too.

She has since come to know the Lord for herself, has given herself wholly to Him with no strings attached, and is one of the most radiant, vivacious young ladies I have ever seen. She is a trophy of God's grace, and we cherish her.

So, gradually we worked our way through all of the frustrations and challenges—with one very painful exception.

My son Alan's search for meaning had led him into a religious cult while attending college. The cult had literally taken control of his life. He didn't think he could make a move without the blessing of his leader, Bagwan Shree Rajneesh.

He had always been a sensitive boy, but his involvement in the cult seemed to have a profound effect on his personality. He was often depressed and lacked any sort of positive drive in his life.

He tried the air force and enjoyed a few years of outstanding achievement and success. Without the steadying hand of the military, however, his return to civilian life led to aimless drifting again.

I tried to talk to him about Jesus, but he didn't seem interested. He was totally wrapped up in his spiritual leader from the Far East.

Then, on October 11, 1984, poor, confused Alan took his own life. His death was in many ways even harder to take than the death of his mother. I knew that Patricia had a real relationship with God, and when she died I knew that I would be able to see her again in the afterlife.

I had no such guarantee about Alan, and all I could do was leave him to God's mercy.

What hurt me even more was that I knew Alan had been seeking after truth—but that he didn't know it when he heard it. His mind had been poisoned by the lie that God is remote and unknowable to man, that religions are futile attempts to bridge this gap, and that one is of no more value than the other. I had tried so hard to reach him, but he just wouldn't listen.

Instead, he went off chasing after some fairy tale, following a leader who promised paradise, but who would deliver only death and sorrow. Alan's death was another terrible blow—and only the grace of God and the support of my wife carried me through that terrible time.

We also received a great deal of love and support from the Christians in our new church home, Christian Chapel in Richmond. We had become members there the previous year, after being less and less satisfied with the church we had attended for years.

We both felt that something was missing there, and we would usually leave the worship services feeling empty and unsatisfied.

We weren't being challenged to reach new levels of spirituality—nor were we being comforted by messages of God's love and grace. We just went along from week to week, allowing church attendance to become more and more a ritual—a duty we owed to God, or a social custom.

We weren't comfortable in that church, and yet we had been there for years. As dissatisfied as we often were, it was home. And it's never easy to leave home and friends.

I would defend the church by telling myself, "I can see why no young person would want to come here . . . but I'm a mature Christian and I can enjoy being in God's house—even if I don't get very much out of the service." It was that kind of reasoning that had allowed my children to come to view Christianity as boring and irrelevant.

Then, one Sunday night when I was on the road, I called Phyllis from my hotel room and found her bubbling over with excitement.

"John, I went to the neatest church this evening!"

"Oh, really?"

"Yes, Christian Chapel. You should have heard the sermon this man preached. I was thrilled!"

She couldn't say enough about the preacher, Brian Guy, or the church. She went on about how the people seemed to be on fire for God—how there was just so much Christian love in this place.

I was glad that Phyllis had enjoyed the service, but I was every bit as skeptical as she was excited. I knew that first impressions can often be misleading. And I didn't know anything about this church—what it stood for or what it really believed.

Still, I agreed that when I got home I would visit the church with her. I wanted to hear this fabulous preacher for myself.

When I went with Phyllis to Christian Chapel, I found out why she was so impressed. Brian was a good preacher, the people did seem to love the Lord, and there was a joyful fellowship. The Sunday service had the feel of a celebration.

We began attending Christian Chapel every once in a while, especially when we felt we needed a spiritual booster shot. Then, one Sunday we enjoyed the morning service so much we decided to go back that evening.

That night, early in the service, Brian asked for prayers from the congregation. And when the man who was sitting behind me started praying, I couldn't believe my ears. He had a deep, resonant voice, and I had never heard anybody pray with such feeling. I almost felt that the Lord Himself was speaking!

The man was giving thanks to the Lord, and it was obviously coming from his heart. It was the kind of prayer that people at Christian Chapel were used to praying. And when other people began to pray, I was overwhelmed by the beautiful simplicity of their prayers—the way they obviously related to God as their loving Father.

I was used to a church where the members sat in their pews, kept their mouths shut, and let the pastor do it all.

Sitting in Christian Chapel that evening was the turning point for me. I decided, "If this church has raised up people who can talk to God the way these people can, then I want to be a part of it."

Phyllis felt exactly the same way, so we decided we would attend Christian Chapel, at least until the end of the year—three months away. And by the end of the year, we realized that we had found the church home we had always needed.

We were delighted to be a part of a church such as Christian Chapel, and we were both growing tremendously in our spiritual lives.

As the years went by, Phyllis and I were growing closer together, and finding that we had more and more in common. I was especially delighted when, two years after we were married, Phyllis discovered flying for herself.

We were in Oshkosh, Wisconsin, when that happened, at the

Experimental Aircraft Association convention, which is the biggest of its kind in the world. Every July, I fly my 1951 Navion lightplane up to Oshkosh, where I indulge myself in hour after hour of aviation history, nostalgia, and technology. Thousands of airplanes are there—every make, model, size, and color, and to someone who loves aviation as much as I do, it's a bit of paradise come to earth.

Phyllis, on the other hand, was forcing herself to smile and be a good sport, while I dragged her up and down lines of airplanes for three days in a row. She would act surprised and interested while I told her some astounding fact I had just discovered which probably didn't mean a thing to her. In fact, she was being so good-humored about it, that I thought she was enjoying it every bit as much as I was. I was wrong. She was smiling and acting interested, even though her feet hurt, her legs ached, and she was bored.

Finally, on the third day of the convention, she told me that she was going to slip into one of the many lecture sessions, and let me go on about my way, walking up and down the two-mile-long lines of vintage airplanes. What she really wanted to do was slip under one of the tents, where it was at least shady, and prop her feet up while she sipped a glass of iced tea.

The session she chose to attend was for "pinch hitters" and was aimed at wives of pilots.

"If you're married to a pilot," the speaker said, "you really ought to know how to land that airplane."

That sounded reasonable.

"You don't think it will happen," he went on, "but what if you're up there in the air and something happens to your husband? Suppose he's unconscious! Would you know how to get that airplane down safely?"

Now he really had her attention.

And the more Phyllis listened, the more she liked what she heard. She had always thought flying was some supertechnical feat that took years of study and practice. But this lecturer made it sound interesting, and even rather simple.

By the time I dropped by the tent to pick her up at the conclusion of the lecture, she was bubbling with excitement.

"Hey!" she said to me, "You don't have to be such a superman to be a pilot! I could do that!"

I laughed. "Of course you could."

I didn't yet understand how serious she was about this. But I found out when, the next day, she insisted upon getting to the airshow by 8:00 A.M. so she could attend the second half of the lecture.

"Eight o'clock!" I protested. "We never get there that early." Ten o'clock sounded about right to me.

But she was insistent. "I *have* to hear the second part of that lecture!"

By the end of part two she was convinced that she could fly. Suddenly it sounded exciting!

As for me, I wasn't going to let any grass grow under my feet. I was going to act before she had a chance to lose interest. Within twenty-four hours of our return to Richmond, Phyllis and I went to the little airport in the nearby town of Henrietta, and Phyllis had her first flying lesson. She loved it, just as I'd known she would. I had been captivated by aviation for nearly forty years, and it was a remarkable feeling to see the woman I loved beginning to be as excited by flying as I am.

She didn't have opportunity to fly all that often, so it took her about a year to get her pilot's license. The day she went up for her solo flight was a very big one for both of us. On that day, I think I learned something of what it must be like for a mother bird, when she finally sees her little ones spread their wings and fly from the nest. Perhaps the analogy doesn't quite fit—but I was very proud, excited, and happy for her.

Then, in the fall of 1981, we were planning to fly, along with some friends, to Oklahoma to attend a retreat held by our friend

Arnold Prater, a Methodist evangelist and author who has had a profound impact on both of our lives.

But at the last moment, the life-style of the airline pilot intervened, and I was suddenly unable to attend. We were both disappointed, because these retreats always help us recharge our spiritual batteries. Then I thought of something—just because I couldn't go was no reason Phyllis couldn't go ahead and take our friends with her.

"Me?" she asked, "Fly? By myself?"

"Why not? You could do it."

She thought for a moment. Then she nodded. "I *could* do it, couldn't I?"

And she did. She flew from Missouri to deep in the Oklahoma hills and back without incident, and the retreat was a fabulous experience.

While Phyllis was discovering the pleasures of flying, I was also continuing to enjoy flying for TWA. By the spring of 1985 I had trained and qualified to fly as captain on the Lockheed L-1011, and I thought I had sufficient seniority to transfer to the international division in New York. The transfer was effective in April, and I began commuting to New York from my home in Missouri.

Airline trips are awarded on the basis of seniority, with the most senior pilot getting his first choice, and the junior man taking whatever is left over. I bid that month for all the L-1011 trip sequences—international first, domestic runs following. (Red-eye specials are always at the bottom of the list.) As a backup choice I bid for several 727 flights in the Mediterranean.

I had flown a few international routes as a flight engineer back in the fifties. But that was on the Constellation, and when the jets came along I wasn't qualified for them, so I hadn't flown any overseas routes since then.

It turned out this time that I didn't have enough seniority to qualify for any of the L-1011 flights. I was given my second choice—flying the 727s in the Mediterranean.

So April found me in Rome, flying between several European and North African cities.

On my first flight over there, a check-pilot came along to guide me around and show me the ropes. Sitting in a hotel in Cairo having dinner, he cautioned me about the dangers of flying in the Middle East.

"You're in a different environment over here, you know," he told me, "and different things can happen to you.

"You're not in Pittsburgh, or Chicago. You've got to be aware of what's going on on the ramps and around your airplane. And just keep your eyes open when you walk through these airports. Be on the lookout for strange characters—for situations that just don't seem right."

I appreciated the advice, but I never really thought that anything out of the ordinary would happen to me. After all, I had been flying with TWA for more than thirty years—over twenty thousand hours—and I had never had any major problems before. I had no reason to think anything was going to happen now.

Yes, I knew that hijackings had occurred . . . and I knew they could happen again. But I didn't think about it any more than anyone else might think about their chances of being involved in an automobile accident. You know the possibility is always there, but you don't think it will ever really happen to you.

During the month of May, my base of operations was switched to Athens, and I flew several flights out of there.

Meanwhile, back home, some unfortunate things were happening in Christian Chapel. A conflict that had been building between Brian and the church elders led to Brian's resignation.

Still, most of the members of the church looked to Brian as their pastor. A large crowd of nearly a hundred people came to a meeting at our house, with Brian present, to discuss what we should do in the future. We were confused, disappointed, and frustrated—and most of us felt that we should begin a new church to carry on the work we had been doing at Christian Chapel.

But Brian had promised the Christian Chapel elders that he would not preach anywhere locally for at least thirty days, so he told us that no decision should be made until after that time. Meanwhile, he urged us to attend other churches in the area. He wanted us to look for things we liked. Then, when we got back together in a month, if we still wanted to start a new church, we could incorporate some of these new ideas into our worship service.

In retrospect, it was a time when the Lord was moving, forcing us out of old, established structures into something new. But still, it was a time of uncertainty and confusion.

This was the situation on June 11, 1985, when Phyllis and I left for Athens, our honeymoon cruise among the Greek islands— and my unscheduled trip into the jaws of terrorism.

4

Terror in the Skies

We've got a hijack."

Those words, spoken by Christian Zimmermann, let me know that what had started out as a routine flight to Rome had suddenly become much more involved. Who were the hijackers? What did they want? How many were there? Would it be possible to overcome them?

I'm sure those same questions were racing through everybody's minds.

I looked over at Christian. He had already gone into action. He reached down and grabbed the fire ax, which is kept by the bulkhead door. Taking the ax out of its holder, he stashed it in a compartment in his desk. He didn't know what sort of weapons the hijackers had, but he didn't want them to have another one. It was extremely quick thinking on his part.

Meanwhile, the banging sound continued . . . and then someone was knocking on the cockpit door.

At first, the knocking was firm, but not violent. But that was followed immediately by a heavy pounding. Whoever was out there meant business. He was not about to give up and just go away.

Then the bottom panel was kicked out of the door, flying several feet into the cockpit.

"Captain, we're being roughed up back here! Please open the door!" It was Uli's voice on the intercom. She was not hysterical, but I could tell she was frightened, and I didn't know what the hijackers might be doing to her.

I turned to Christian. "Go ahead and open the door!"

He unlocked the door and began to open it. But before he had a chance, two young men burst into the cockpit. At least one of them was waving around a large-bore automatic pistol as he yelled his demands.

"*Algera! Algera!*" he screamed.

Because of his thick Arabic accent I couldn't understand what he was saying. I turned to look at him, and he thrust his gun into my face.

"*Algera!*" he screamed again.

This time, I caught on.

"Oh, you mean Algiers?"

"*Algera!*"

"Okay," I said. "We'll take you to Algiers. Whatever you want. Just don't get excited."

It wasn't the gun that frightened me, but the other guy was carrying a couple of hand grenades and also what looked like a plastic bomb. If he let one of those grenades go off, there was no telling how many people might be killed and hurt—and there was also the possibility of a crash.

Our hijackers were two young men, probably in their late teens or early twenties. They were well-groomed, average-looking guys who didn't look like they could be hijackers or killers. But I could see right away that they were extremely nervous and hyper. They knew that what they were doing was highly illegal and dangerous—that it was just the two of them against the other 150 of us on the plane—and they were determined to do whatever they had to do to maintain control.

They kept bursting in and out of the cockpit, then running up and down the aisles, occasionally banging passengers on the head to show that they meant business. At that time, of course, we didn't know for sure how many hijackers there were. The truth was that there were to have been three of them, but the third member of their group had been unable to obtain a seat at the airport in Athens.

As soon as they left the cockpit, Phil got on the radio to report the fact that we were being hijacked.

When he had completed his transmission, we looked at each other for a moment, wondering what would come next.

"Looks like we're going to Algiers," I said.

He looked puzzled. "But where is Algiers?"

"Beats me. It's on the coast of North Africa, west of here somewhere. That's about all I know."

Phil began shuffling through his charts, trying to find something on Algiers. When he finally found it, we had to figure out how far it was and whether we had enough fuel to get there.

We didn't. We had seventeen thousand pounds on board. That was enough fuel to get us to Rome, but if we headed for Algeria, we'd end up ditching somewhere in the sea.

How did we communicate that to these guys? And even if we did, would they believe us?

When the leader of the two—the young man with the gun—came back into the cockpit, I tried to tell him we couldn't possibly make it to Algiers.

"No Algiers," I said, in Pidgin English. "No fuel."

He looked at me blankly. "*Algera*," he said.

I pointed at the fuel gauge and tried hand signals to show him what I was talking about. He was unmoved.

"*Algera!*"

He had apparently been trained in hijack school—and these guys were highly trained—that airline captains were devious sorts who would lie to you and attempt to play tricks on you.

But the stubbornness of this young man was beginning to get to me. He was just a kid—and I'm a mature command pilot. Besides all of that, this was *my* airplane, and it made me angry that this punk was trying to tell me what I could and could not do with it. I knew its capabilities and I knew its limitations.

He waved his gun in my face again. "*Algera!*" Was that the only word this kid knew?

Suddenly the whole situation just got to me.

"Listen!" I snapped. "If you want to keep going this way, I'll put you in the ocean somewhere off the coast of Tunis! Because that's where I'm going to run out of fuel!"

My sudden outburst of anger made him realize that I wasn't kidding. He seemed to understand, and he was at least willing to compromise.

During all of this, I was trying to talk to the hijackers in Pidgin English. But about this time we discovered, somehow, that one of them spoke fluent German. That was a good break, because Uli also speaks German and was able to translate back and forth.

With her help, I got them to accept Cairo as a new destination. Cairo wasn't nearly as far as Algiers, and I figured we could make it that far without any problems. We'd be able to get fuel there, and then we'd resume the flight to Algiers.

So, once again Phil began going through his charts, plotting a course for Cairo, while the two hijackers babbled excitedly in Arabic.

They were apparently having second thoughts about Cairo. They knew that Cairo's airport has very tight security, and it was no sure bet as a safe haven for them. Beyond that, they didn't know what kind of reception they'd get in Egypt.

The one with the gun let us know they'd changed their minds.

"*Byeroot!*" he yelled. "*Byeroot!* Fuel only!"

I looked at Christian, and he looked at me. We both looked at Phil. None of us understood what the hijacker was saying.

Suddenly it dawned on me. "I think they want to go to Beirut."

The other hijacker nodded. *"Byeroot."*

That was fine with me. I knew that Beirut was just a short distance north of Tel Aviv, and since Tel Aviv was the same distance from Athens as Rome, I knew we had the fuel to fly there. Maybe once we got them where they wanted to go, they'd be on their way and leave the rest of us alone. Anyway, it would be much safer on the ground than it was up here, flying around aimlessly, with nowhere to go.

Once again, we changed directions, banking back toward the Mediterranean's eastern shore. Suddenly, a devious thought came to me. I wondered if I might be able to sneak these guys into Tel Aviv, with them thinking we were landing in Beirut. I'd have to think some more about that.

But almost immediately, as if they knew what I had been thinking, one of the hijackers asked to speak to Beirut on the radio. I tried to explain to him that we were still more than six hundred miles from Beirut, and that we would have to be within two hundred miles before we could talk to the tower there. He seemed to believe me and be satisfied that I was telling the truth. Both of them appeared to trust me more since I had lost my temper with them.

But they didn't understand entirely, because every five minutes or so, they would again ask to talk to *"Byeroot."* Well, so much for my idea about Tel Aviv.

As we plotted our course for Beirut, the hijackers seemed to be becoming more hyper and more violent. When they had first entered the cockpit, they had looked directly at the crash ax holder and demanded to know where it was. Christian had told them we didn't have one. We soon discovered why they wanted it. Using the kicked-out door panel as a club, one of them methodically smashed the doorknob and lock completely off the cockpit door, leaving a gaping hole where it had been.

This allowed the door to swing freely and prevented us from locking them out of the cockpit. One of them then wrenched one of the arms off Christian's flight engineer's seat, while the other hijacker, having bound one of the young military servicemen tightly, brought him forward and dumped him through the open cockpit doorway. The chair arm was then used as a club with which to severely beat him.

They also continued running up and down the aisle of the airplane, banging passengers on both sides of the aisle with the butts of their guns. Then they would run into the cockpit and give Christian a couple of whacks.

They left me pretty much alone, but poor Christian had the misfortune of sitting closest to the cockpit door. They would run in, reach over, and give him a solid crack on the shoulder or on the head. Then they'd run out and we'd hear the cracking noises as the passengers were being whacked.

We found out later that they made the passengers bend over, keeping their heads down in a terribly uncomfortable position, for hours on end. Those who had trouble maintaining that position were singled out for especially violent treatment.

One elderly woman was having a particularly tough time keeping her head down. Finally, she couldn't take it anymore and straightened up to try to relieve the pain in her back. Immediately, one of the hijackers jumped on her back with both feet, smashing her face down into her lap and breaking her glasses in the process.

I don't know why they didn't beat on me. Perhaps it was out of respect for my position as the captain. Maybe they figured that I was so frail and elderly I would collapse if they laid a finger on me! Or maybe it was just because it was easier to keep hitting Christian, since he was easier to reach.

Once in a while, they would reach up and pop Phil a good one, but for the most part poor Christian was their whipping boy, and after a while, he was a mess. Blood trickled down his face from a cut on his forehead, and bloodstains on his shirt showed the other places where they had beat him.

As the hijackers ran back out of the cockpit after giving him a particularly nasty blow, I looked at him, not knowing what to say. I wanted to give him some encouragement, but what could I say in a situation like this?

He gave me a rueful little smile.

"Well," he said, "it looks like we have a strong friend up there looking out for us!"

For a second, I looked up through the overhead windows of the cockpit, expecting to see a United States fighter plane soaring above us. Instead, all I saw was blue sky.

I looked back at Christian, not understanding what he was talking about. He pointed at the little Holy Spirit pin I was wearing on my tie.

"That's the Friend I mean."

"Oh, you bet!" I answered. "I'll say amen to that!"

That was the first time I realized that he was a Christian. Up until that point, in fact, I had been calling him Chris, but now I realized that he wanted to be called by his full name—Christian—for a very special reason. It was a great comfort to know that we both had a deep belief in Christ.

Now that we at least knew where we were going, I hoped our captors would relax and take it a little easier on us. But, if anything, they seemed to step up their attacks. They made it clear, speaking to Uli in German and to the rest of us in broken English, that they were on a suicide mission, and that they would not be hesitant to die for their cause—although we still had no idea what that cause might be.

They also made it clear that not only did they not care if they died, but they didn't care if any of the rest of us died either!

As we flew past Cyprus, we were finally able to make radio contact with Beirut. The Beirut controller responded to us just as I had thought he would. He didn't want to have anything to do with us and told us the airport was closed.

73

But Phil replied that we didn't care if they were closed or not. We were going to land there because we had no choice.

"These people are armed and dangerous," he said. "And they are ordering us to land at Beirut."

"I am sorry," came the reply, "but we are closed, and you will not be allowed to land."

I broke in, "My aircraft is in distress, I am low on fuel, and I am declaring an emergency. I demand clearance to land at Beirut." The controller asked us to stand by, saying that he would try to arrange it. I continued the descent straight for the airport which was becoming plainly visible in the clear morning light.

Leveling off at landing pattern altitude, we went through the landing checklists, then turned on to final approach, passing the tall buildings of downtown Beirut. The controller then said, in a somewhat plaintive and frustrated tone, "Very well, sir, you are cleared to land. Land quietly please."

I did not know what the last remark meant, probably nothing—the controller was under a great deal of stress. In any event, we made a normal landing.

Once we had landed in Beirut, the hijackers made me stop in the middle of the runway. They then got on the radio with the tower and a long, excited conversation in Arabic ensued. We had no idea what was being discussed, but the hijackers did not seem happy. They were apparently not getting the response they wanted or expected from the tower.

Finally, a Follow-Me truck came out onto the runway to lead us to the refueling area. But the hijacker with the gun leaned out the cockpit window and began waving his gun around, and the truck drove off. The hijackers were insisting, apparently, that fuel be brought out to the airplane. They did not want us to taxi into the refueling area because they were afraid of an ambush.

As I began to understand what was going on, I talked to the gunman and explained as patiently as I could that we would have to taxi into the refueling area. It was the only way we could possibly get fuel—and thus the only means of getting to Algiers.

At last, he seemed to understand. I would be allowed to taxi to the refueling area. But he was going to make sure that I didn't try any "funny" business. As I taxied down the runway, he stood in back of me, with his cocked pistol held against my head. In his other hand, he held a hand grenade, with its pin pulled, directly in front of my face.

As if the distractions weren't bad enough, his hand in front of my face made it nearly impossible to see where I was going. I figured that all I had to do was hit one chuckhole, and it would be the end of the ride for everybody.

It was at this time that the thought first crossed my mind that all of us could very well be dead within the next five minutes. I hadn't really thought about it before, but now it seemed very likely that that's what would happen. But right behind that thought, before I even had a chance to get nervous, another thought entered my head.

Well, that wouldn't be so bad. Because if I die, I'll get to see Jesus!

From that moment on, the peace of God flooded into my being. Suddenly, I was not afraid—and I can honestly say I never experienced another moment of fear during the seventeen-day ordeal that followed. I experienced worry and anxiety, yes, over the well-being of the passengers and wondering how Phyllis and the rest of the family were coping with the situation. But I was never again afraid for my own safety.

I knew that if God didn't want me to die, there was nothing the hijackers could do to kill me. He would see to it that the grenade didn't go off or that the trigger didn't get pulled. If He did allow me to die—well, He knows best, and everything goes according to His plan.

Looking back on it now, I'm amazed. The typical human impulse would have been to go to pieces—but God was there in a real, tangible way, and He kept me strong!

However, things were not going any better. Once we made it safely into the refueling area, the hijackers became angry when no one came immediately to bring us fuel. They resumed beating the young serviceman, who was later identified as Robert Stethem, a navy diver.

The sounds of the blows were sickening, as they brought the chair arm down on Stethem again and again and again. We wanted to stop it—would have given anything to be able to stop it—but knew that there was nothing any of us could do.

I wondered why they were dealing so harshly with him. He hadn't done anything to them. Perhaps they just wanted us to know they meant business, but there was much more to it than that. It seemed to me that they actually hated this young man. Maybe it was because he represented the United States government—and they were very expressive in their hatred of the United States.

As their blows crashed down on Stethem again and again, Phil got on the radio.

"They're beating the passengers! They're beating the passengers!" he cried. "We demand fuel!"

Eventually, there was a response and workmen arrived to give us the fuel we needed.

Because the arrival of the fuel seemed to lessen tensions somewhat, I figured it was a good time to seek the release of some of our passengers. It was also true that with all that fuel we were several thousand pounds overweight, and I wanted to relieve that situation, too.

"Don't you think you ought to let the women and children go?" I asked the young man with the gun. "You don't need them. It's not going to hurt you to let them go."

I tried to explain to him that we were overloaded, and that it would be wise to let some people go for that reason. But he just looked at me blankly, as if he didn't understand a word I was saying—and perhaps he didn't. Conversation with these fellows wasn't the easiest thing in the world.

At least I had tried.

But as the hijacker walked away from me and went back into

the cabin to check on conditions there, Uli Derickson was waiting for him, and the two of them began conversing in German. I discovered later that Uli was taking up the same issue, pleading with him to allow the women and children to go free.

She apparently was more convincing than I had been. Our captors finally agreed to let nineteen passengers—seventeen women and two children—leave the plane. It wasn't much, really, but it was something.

We flew from Beirut shortly before one-thirty in the afternoon, headed for Algiers, some four hours away. Had everything gone according to plan, our short trip to Rome would have been over, and we would have been headed back to Athens. I wondered where Phyllis was, and if she had heard about the hijacking. I hoped she was okay and that she wasn't too worried.

I also hoped that things would go well in Algiers. Surely, once we got there, the hijackers would explain why they had hijacked the plane in the first place. Perhaps they would issue a statement or two designed to focus world attention on their "problem," and then they would let us go back to Athens. I still had no idea what had begun here!

As we approached Algiers, we ran into a problem off the coast of Tunisia. Word came from Tunis that we would not be allowed to enter into Tunisian airspace—and would be shot down if we attempted to do so. That turn of events forced us to stay out over the Mediterranean and fly along the coast of North Africa. That was no major problem in itself, but it showed me something: We were tainted, like a disease—nobody wanted anything at all to do with us.

As we got closer to Algiers, the hijackers began to get on the radio and make long, passionate speeches in Arabic. We figured they were making their demands, but we had no idea what they were saying. Their attitudes let us know, though, that they weren't meeting with a great deal of success. Nobody seemed to be receptive to their demands.

The people in Algiers were just like everybody else. They

didn't want us in their territory and wished we would just go away.

"The airport is closed," said the heavily accented voice on the radio. "You will not be allowed to land."

Phil shot back, "We are going to land. We have no choice. They have told us they will blow up the airplane if we do not land in Algiers!"

He also explained that we had to land at Algiers because we did not have enough fuel to go anywhere else, even if the hijackers would allow it.

After a few minutes, the Algerian controller agreed to open a runway for us. But we still didn't know what to expect. As we made our final descent into the airport, we could see that the place was virtually covered by Algerian military personnel and armored vehicles. For all we knew, we could be blasted out of the sky. What was more likely, though, was that a raid on the airplane would be staged. I hoped not, because I knew that if such a raid was attempted, many innocent people would be killed. I was still hoping we could get out of this without anyone being killed or seriously injured.

We sat on the ground in Algiers for several hours while the hijackers discussed their demands with airport officials.

We still didn't know what they were after, until Uli told us they were saying something about wanting Lebanese hostages in Israel to be released. What Lebanese hostages? None of us had any idea who or what they were talking about, but we all experienced the same sinking feeling. This was no ordinary, run-of-the-mill hijacking. We were being held for ransom. We would be set free only in exchange for those who were being held by Israel.

There were a great many conversations going on at this time, but since all of them were in Arabic, we could only speculate about the content. We did know that our captors were threatening to start shooting the passengers unless Algerian officials would meet with them to discuss their demands. Those threats brought groups of Algerian officials to the airplane to negotiate with the hijackers through the cockpit windows. At one point a man came onto the airplane to speak directly to the hijackers. We were told that he was the president of Algeria, and maybe he was. We never found out for sure.

Whatever was going on wasn't making our captors happy. Instead of relaxing they were becoming more abusive and violent. They brought army Major Kurt Carlson into the cockpit tightly bound and dumped him on the floor. They began beating him savagely, all the while demanding fuel so we could fly somewhere else—where, we didn't know.

When the Algerians would not agree to give us fuel, the hijackers stepped up their threats to start killing passengers. When it became apparent that the threats were not made lightly, airport officials relented and sent a fuel truck out to us.

When the fuel truck arrived, the hijacker with the hand grenades leaned out of one of the cockpit windows to talk to the driver. The two of them were having an animated discussion in Arabic, and as the conversation continued, the hijacker leaned farther and farther out the window.

One push—one very slight push—and we could be minus one hijacker. I looked over at Christian. As his eyes met mine, I knew that he was thinking the same thing. Our eyes locked for a few seconds as we considered whether it was worth a try.

In two seconds, we could have grabbed that guy's legs and tossed him about forty feet onto the runway below. I wanted to do it so badly I could hardly restrain myself.

I glanced back over my shoulder. There was the other hijacker, with his gun drawn, watching over the passengers in the cabin.

I turned back to Christian and saw the look of resignation in his eyes. We both knew we couldn't do it. There was no doubt in my mind that if we tried, the other hijacker would begin shooting passengers at random. They had told us they didn't care if any of us had to die—and I believed them. It just wasn't worth the risk.

After a few more tempting minutes, the hijacker pulled his head back inside the cockpit and strode off, as if he had more important matters to attend to. But whatever the topic of their conversation had been, the truck driver didn't think it was over. He began yelling about something, although we didn't know what.

Phil stuck his head out the window. Then he pulled it back in.

"He's asking me for something."

"What?" I asked.

"I don't know. I can't understand him!"

Phil leaned out the window again. "Tell me again what you want!"

I strained to understand the reply, but I could not make out what the man was saying.

"What?" Phil asked again. This time, he thought he understood.

The look on his face was a strange combination of amazement, amusement, and exasperation. "You know what?" he exclaimed. "I think this guy is asking for a credit card!"

I leaned back in my chair and rolled my eyes skyward. "A credit card! You mean he wants us to pay for fuel so we can hijack ourselves?"

"I'm sure that's what he's asking for," Phil answered.

I looked over at Christian, who just shook his head as if he were dumbfounded.

Uli Derickson stuck her head into the cockpit to see what was going on.

"Uli," I said, "you'll never guess what this idiot out here wants! He's asking for a credit card!"

Uli looked at me for a second or two as if she hadn't heard me right. "A credit card?"

She put her hand to her forehead and let loose with a half-hysterical laugh.

"He wants a credit card? I'll give him a credit card!" She walked out of the cockpit for a minute and came back with her purse. "He wants a credit card!" she mumbled to herself as she rummaged through it.

She finally found what she was looking for.

"If he really wants one, give him this." She held up her Shell Oil credit card.

Phil took it and handed it out the window. It was exactly what the man wanted! Once he had Uli's card, he began pumping fuel: Six thousand gallons at a dollar per gallon, and all on Uli's Shell credit card!

Meanwhile, they had dragged Kurt Carlson back to his seat—and resumed their abuse of Stethem, the navy diver. He was tied up, brought forward, and beaten until he was left lying unconscious in the doorway. Again, the beatings were terribly savage, and if I had had a gun, I would not have hesitated to shoot both hijackers right there.

Young Stethem was an incredibly brave young man. He didn't cry out once as they were beating on him. He wouldn't give them the satisfaction.

It was during this stop in Algiers that I first became aware of the wild mood swings and twisted thinking of our hijackers. For example, they had beaten Carlson and Stethem mercilessly, swearing at them all the while. And yet they let an additional twenty-one passengers leave the aircraft for "humanitarian reasons." While they were attempting, on the one hand, to show the rest of the world they weren't such savages, they were, on the other hand, constantly threatening to begin shooting the remaining passengers one at a time if their demands weren't met.

All of us in the cockpit quickly became aware that our kidnappers were totally unpredictable. There was no telling at all what they might do next.

Once we had a planeload of fuel, we took off again. We didn't know, until we were airborne, that we were going back to Beirut. Once we were told that, we knew that our hijackers didn't really have a game plan. They'd known what to do to get this far—but not what to do afterward.

For all we knew, we could be shuttling back and forth between Beirut and Algiers for days to come!

As we were flying, if the hijackers were in the cockpit, they would not allow us to talk on the radio. If we tried, they would cut us off.

"Don't talk! Don't talk!"

They were apparently afraid that we were trying to set up some sort of a trap. Meanwhile, we were probably just as concerned about a raid by the Delta Force as they were. We were aware that any such rescue attempt would result in heavy casualties, and that was something we were trying to avoid.

The aim of the Delta Force is to enter an airplane with lightning quickness, using sharpshooters to bring down the terrorists. But in this instance, even if they had been able to carry out every step of a raid with total perfection, many passengers still could have been killed. The reason? The hijacker with the hand grenades was constantly popping the safety pins out. I think he had the pins out of them more often than they were in. It was nerve-wracking watching him play with those things!

So even if a sharpshooter had managed to shoot the hijackers before they could get off any shots, what about those hand grenades? What if one of the pins had been pulled out? The hijackers would fall to the floor dead. The terror would appear to be over. But a few seconds later, the hand grenade would explode, killing many passengers.

If the hijackers had both been armed merely with guns, it might have been possible for us to overpower them at some point. But those hand grenades were our major worry.

We tried hard to persuade the hijackers that there were occasions when we absolutely had to get on the radio, but they simply did not understand. On one particular occasion, one air traffic controller was trying to contact us while the hijackers were standing in the cockpit.

His voice kept coming through my headset. "Flight 847, state your position!" "TWA Flight 847, state your position!"

As soon as the hijackers left the cockpit to check on things back in the cabin, I got on the radio.

"I will talk when I can talk!" I snapped. "Otherwise, do not try to contact me!"

We tried to do all of our talking on the radio when the hijackers were out of the cockpit, but more than once we had to cut off things in the middle of a conversation to keep from being caught.

By the time we made it back to Beirut, it was nearly two-thirty in the morning. We had been in the cockpit for more than sixteen hours in an extremely tense situation. I had been awake for more than twenty hours, the hijackers hadn't allowed me to get out of my chair except for quick trips to the lavatory, and I was totally exhausted.

At one point, when I had really begun feeling the tension in my back, I stood up and tried to stretch. Immediately, a hijacker was waving his gun at me and saying, "No! No!" He motioned for me to get back in my seat. I had had about enough of this foolishness and I glared at him.

"Hey!" I said. "I'm an old grandfather! I . . . ahhhh . . . my back hurts!"

When he saw that I was becoming angry, and when he heard me speak of being an old grandfather, he changed his mind. "Okay! Okay!"

It was the same old pattern. If you spoke sharply to them, they could act almost like school kids who had been caught in some form of mischief . . . who were sorry. But then at other times, they could be absolutely unfeeling and brutal—as we were soon to find out.

We were getting no cooperation from the Beirut control tower.

"I am sorry but the airport is closed. You will not be allowed to land."

The controller informed us that barricades had been set up on the runways to keep us away. Any attempt at a landing would result in a crash.

Normally, it is the first officer's job to handle the radio communication, but I got on to see if I could convince them to remove the barricades.

"I'm exhausted," I said. "My airplane is in distress . . . we're in deadly danger. I implore you to open your airport and let us land!"

"I sympathize with you, sir," came the controller's reply. "But unfortunately my superiors do not care about your problems."

I turned to one of the hijackers.

"The runways are closed," I explained. "If we try to land, we will crash the airplane."

His eyes showed no flicker of emotion. "Good!" he said. "That will save us the trouble of blowing it up!"

I got back on the radio and told the controller I had no choice. If there were barricades on the runways, we would just smash into them. We were coming in.

I called Uli over and told her to prepare the passengers for a crash landing.

"We're doing everything we can to get the airport open," I told her. "But you'd better get the passengers prepared, just in case."

I began circling as communications with the tower continued.

"You'll have to wait a little while," he told me. "But if you give me some time, I'll try to get the runway cleared."

While we circled overhead, a war was being waged on the runways beneath us. Lebanon is a country torn by civil war, and whether or not we would be allowed to land had become an issue in that war.

Thankfully for TWA Flight 847 and everyone on board, the side that was in favor of allowing us to land won this particular skirmish. After we circled a few more times, the Beirut tower gave us the good news: The barricades had been removed, and we were being cleared for landing.

The first thing I did was to get on the public address system and tell the passengers that our landing in Beirut would be normal. That was the first piece of good news any of them had had in quite a while!

The landing was still not going to be routine. The airport had been shot to pieces in the war and the regular instrument landing system had been destroyed. Because of this, we were forced to make an old-fashioned low-frequency-beacon approach. With the shot-up condition of the tower, we were lucky that the low-frequency beacon was operating.

The danger of the landing was complicated by the fact that all of us in the cockpit were beyond exhaustion. We had reached the point where this whole thing didn't even seem real. We were exhausted almost to the point of being beyond caring.

There on the floor behind us, still unconscious after being beaten mercilessly, lay Robbie Stethem. No, this couldn't be real. It had to be some terrible nightmare.

After we touched down, the hijackers ordered me to stop the airplane in the middle of the runway. They did not want to get too close to any buildings or obstacles that might serve as hiding places for would-be rescuers.

As we sat there, the hijackers began a lengthy discussion with the tower in Arabic. Whatever was being discussed, they weren't getting the answers they wanted. Their voices grew louder, angrier, and more threatening until they were practically screaming into the radio.

Suddenly, one of them turned back to where young Stethem lay, still unconscious, on the floor. He jerked Stethem to his feet, and pushed him into the open doorway.

A single shot rang out, and Stethem's body fell to the pavement below.

Phil yelled into the radio, "They've just killed a passenger! They've just killed a passenger!"

"How terrible!" came the reply from the tower. "That you would kill an innocent passenger!" The controller was attempting to embarrass and shame the hijackers—but they showed no remorse at all over what they had done and threatened to kill another passenger if their demands were not met immediately.

I cannot describe how I felt when Stethem was killed. There was just a heavy, heavy sadness that washed over me. I leaned forward in my seat and closed my eyes. I didn't pray, because I didn't know what to say. They had killed him—and I couldn't do anything to change that—but the sadness and anger I felt were indescribable.

Immediately, the gunman was back in the cockpit, waving his weapon around and demanding that I taxi into the refueling area. As I began moving down the runway I turned the wheels sharply to avoid running over the young serviceman's body.

We spent the remainder of the night sitting in the refueling area. We were allowed only a few minutes' sleep here and there, sitting in our cockpit chairs.

It wasn't until much later that we came to understand what was going on during the brief stop on the runway in Beirut—what the hijackers wanted and why they became so angry. They killed Stethem partly because to them he represented the hated United States military. Additionally, they were demanding that the Amal militia become involved in the hijacking and were enraged when the Amal leadership had not responded.

To understand what was going on, you have to understand a little bit about the reasons for the civil war in Lebanon.

When Lebanon obtained its independence from France, in 1944, the majority of the country's citizens were Maronite Christians, with Sunnite Moslems a close second. And so, power was apportioned accordingly. The president must be a Christian, whereas the prime minister, who is second in command, is a Sunnite Moslem, and so on.

However, in the years since 1944, the Shi'ite Moslems have become the majority in Lebanon, but they are still virtually without political power.

There are other reasons for the fighting going on in Lebanon today, but one of the primary causes is that the Shi'ites want to have a bigger say in the government of their country.

The Shi'ites themselves are divided into several parties, the largest being the Amal. *Amal* means "hope," and as might be gathered from that name, they are the more moderate, more pragmatic group. One of the other large Shi'ite parties is the

Hisbollah, or Party of God. The Hisbollah are extremist in nature and look to Iran's Ayatollah Khomeini as their example. (Iran is also a predominantly Shi'ite nation.)

It was the Hisbollah that had plotted and carried out the hijacking of TWA Flight 847.

To put it in perspective, Shi'ite Moslems, who make up less than 15 percent of the world's total Moslem population, are the most violently anti-Western people in the Middle East. And the Hisbollah are among the most violently anti-Western of the Shi'ites.

They are a less-disciplined group, with a small power base, whereas the Amal Party is large, influential, and led by Nabih Berri, a man of considerable stature in Lebanon. The Beirut airport is in an area of the city that is controlled by Amal militiamen, so what the hijackers demanded, as we sat on the runway there, was to have some of the Amal soldiers join them on the plane. When someone balked at that idea—who I don't know— they shot Stethem to prove that they would not take no for an answer, and Berri later said that he had entered the negotiations in order to prevent further bloodshed.

Within half an hour of taxiing to the refueling area, our captors got their wish, and five more terrorists joined us on board the aircraft. I can't say that I was happy to see them, but at the same time, I thought if their presence would cause the original hijackers to relax, it was a good thing to have them on board.

As we sat there in the darkness, a Red Cross ambulance and Lebanese officials in three cars searched the runway with their headlights until they found and removed the body of Robert Stethem.

Shortly before dawn, the hijackers told us that we were going to take off again. They had heard rumors that an Israeli strike force was approaching the Beirut coast, and they wanted to get out of there.

Before we took off, Middle East Airlines delivered boxes of

sandwiches and bottles of water to the plane. At least we would have something to eat.

Where were we headed this time? Back to Algiers.

Now flying from Athens to Beirut hadn't been too hard, because TWA flies regularly into Tel Aviv, and I knew that Beirut was just north of Tel Aviv. But getting back to Algiers was another matter. In looking at our charts, we had discovered that there are no airways between Beirut and Algiers, because nobody flies between those two points.

We knew, too, that flying nonstop between Beirut and Algiers was stretching a 727 to its maximum capability. We wouldn't have enough fuel to allow for any errors in our navigation.

What I finally did was to take a chart of the entire Mediterranean area. I made a crease on one side at Beirut, and another crease on the other side at Algiers, and then I folded it across my leg, connecting the two points.

The charts are laid out in such a way that a straight line drawn on them is a great circle navigation route, which is the shortest distance between two points. So that was the course line we followed to Algiers. It wasn't really high tech . . . but it worked!

Our arrival in Algiers was uneventful, and shortly after we landed, a doctor was allowed to come on board to see how the passengers were doing. Three passengers were allowed to leave the aircraft after he determined that they were in serious trouble because of the heat—and it was hot, sitting there on the runway with the North African sun blazing down on us.

Meanwhile, the hijackers were back on the radio, restating their demand for the release of the Lebanese citizens they said were being held in Israel. They also demanded that the other member of the original group of hijackers, who had been detained by Greek authorities, be brought to the airplane. If he were not brought to the plane, they said, they would kill all of the Greek passengers on board, and there were several.

They also took every opportunity to denounce America. They blamed America for just about every evil in the world. Why is there hunger? America's fault. Poverty? Again, America's fault. I was surprised that they didn't blame America for chicken pox and measles!

We had been sitting on the runway for nearly twelve hours when the third member of the original hijacking group, Ali Atweh, was finally brought to the plane. Apparently, Algerian officials had used him as a bargaining chip in their attempts to get other passengers off the plane. When Atweh came on board, more than fifty passengers and the five flight attendants were released.

All of the hostages left on board the plane now were American men. All the women, children, and citizens of other countries had been released.

This was another indication of the hijackers' strategy. They wanted Israel to release prisoners it was holding, but they saw the United States as the real key to their fellow countrymen's release, because of our supposed control of Israel.

Once Atweh came on board, we found out that he was a master at stealing. It seemed as though he took it as his mission in life to rob everyone, and he did a pretty thorough job of it. He started off by going through the cabin and taking everything he could get from the passengers—wedding rings, wallets, you name it, he took it.

Back in the cabin, we watched the terrorists going through the overhead bins, looking for things to steal. They would take a bag out of the overhead bin and begin throwing everything out of it onto the floor. If they wanted something, they'd set it aside or stuff it into their pockets. If they didn't want something, they would just toss it onto the floor. Then, when the bag was empty, it, too, would be tossed on the floor and they'd move on to the next one.

I watched one of them going through someone's wallet. He opened it to the photo section and then pulled out all the photos one at a time. He would look at a photo for a few seconds and then throw it over his shoulder. He'd look at the next one for a while, and then it, too, would be tossed over his shoulder.

Credit cards went onto the floor with the trash. They apparently didn't know what they were. They didn't understand what checks were either.

One of them was looking through Phil's checkbook.

"What is this?"

"It's a check."

"What is a check?"

Phil tried to explain it to him, but he still didn't seem to understand.

"Show me."

So Phil took out his pen, wrote out a check for two thousand dollars and gave it to the guy.

That night, we were able to get our first "real" sleep, stretched out over a row of seats in the cabin. It wasn't much, but after the events of the last two days, it felt like a king-size bed!

The next morning, the hijackers woke us up early and told us we were going to be leaving Algiers again.

There was a new leader by this time—a man in his early thirties who was giving orders to all the others—and the attitude had changed considerably. Among the other things we were thankful for was the fact that this new leader spoke fluent English and seemed to be better educated than the others. It was good to have someone in charge with whom we could readily communicate. He would not tell us his real name—none of them would—but went by the alias Jihad.

We needed fuel again, and the original hijackers had always been able to get fuel by saying they were going to start shooting the passengers. This time, the attitude had changed completely.

Jihad came into the cockpit followed by a couple of his men. With them was one of the young passengers.

"We want to play a little game here," he said. "We need to convince the airport to bring us fuel."

He went on to explain that they were going to open the microphone, and that the young passenger had agreed to cry out as if he were being beaten. This, it was hoped, would prompt quick delivery of the fuel we needed.

Unfortunately, though, this particular passenger wasn't much of an actor. He gave out a couple of halfhearted cries that barely made their way out over the radio.

Phil gave him a disdainful look. "Hey! I can do better than that."

"Then go ahead!" Jihad prompted him.

Phil immediately cut loose with some of the most bloodcurdling screams I have ever heard. Perhaps it was good therapy for Phil, letting out some of the tensions of the last few terrible days. Whatever, I discovered that Phil is one of the all-time champion screamers. You would have thought the poor guy was being beaten within an inch of his life!

As Phil continued to scream, Jihad turned to me.

"Please open the window."

When I did, he took out his chrome-plated pistol and squeezed off three or four quick shots out the window.

The sound of those shots being fired also went out over the radio.

Actually, we rather enjoyed this little episode. It sounds bizarre, but it was a release from the tension—and we were relieved that they didn't seem inclined to start beating passengers again.

Our little drama worked, too. The fuel truck arrived within minutes to fill our tanks. But it was the same driver who had fueled us up the day before . . . and he asked again for a credit card.

Phil leaned out the window and shouted down at him, "Hey, buddy! Don't give us that! We gave you our credit card yesterday!"

When he realized he wasn't going to get another credit card out of us, he went ahead and pumped in the fuel.

I turned back to Jihad.

"Where do you want to go today?"

He wouldn't tell me.

"Listen," I said, "if you're wanting to go a long distance away, I need to know so I can figure out if we can get there."

He nodded, and I continued. "If I can do it, I'll take you wherever you want to go. But if I can't, I can't."

"Well, we want to go to Aden."

I had no idea, really, where Aden was, except that it was down on the southern end of the Arabian peninsula. But when we got the charts out and started checking, we found it was nearly three thousand miles away. The only way we could possibly get to Aden was to stop in Cairo to refuel.

"What if we refuel in Beirut and fly from there to Aden?" he asked.

"No, that won't work. Beirut is much farther north than Cairo, and we couldn't make it all the way from Beirut to Aden without a stop in between."

The terrorists began talking among themselves in Arabic. It was obvious that they were trying to come up with a new game plan. I didn't know what they were talking about, but I was sure I heard the word *Tehran* mentioned more than once. And, though I didn't care that much where else we went, I definitely didn't want to fly into Iran!

Finally, their conversation ended, and Jihad told us, "Okay, we will fly back to Beirut for fuel. Then we will go somewhere else."

On the flight back to Beirut, the hijackers were much more relaxed and allowed us to use the radio pretty much as we wished. We were constantly guarded, but usually by three inexperienced militiamen who obviously didn't speak English and didn't care how much we talked on the radio.

I looked over at Phil and Christian. "We have to find some way to stop this flying."

"I know," they both responded. It was obvious to all of us that the hijackers were fresh out of ideas and were just fumbling about without a real plan of attack.

While we were all thinking and talking about ways we could stop the flying, I decided to use the radio and see if I could get anybody to answer a couple of questions. As we were passing over Malta I got on the radio and tried to raise the company station in Rome. I was not able to make contact, but a 747 passing through the area did pick us up, and since that pilot had high-frequency radio contact with New York, I used him for a link.

"Hey," I said, "I think these guys might want to go to Tehran. Would you call back to New York and have them check with the State Department and get me the answer to two questions?"

He said he would.

"Question one is, if we take them to Tehran, will they be safe there? Will they find some kind of a haven?

"The second question is, if we fly into Tehran, will we be allowed to leave?" Since the hijackers had struck out on every ground stop so far, I thought they might be looking for a convenient exit from their dilemma. I was going to propose the Tehran stop as a way of getting rid of them. But before I could get the answers to my questions, the 747 was out of range.

After a while, I got back on the radio and contacted Athens, asking the same two questions. This time, someone came back on with a technical question about whether we had enough fuel to fly to Tehran.

That irritated me. I thought, *Here I have all these problems . . . and I know how to draw up a flight plan between point A and point B. I don't need advice on that—but I do need to know about the political ramifications!"*

The people in Athens started suggesting that I land at Larnaca instead of Beirut. I had no idea why they were making such suggestions, until I found out later that the Delta Force had been moved to Larnaca. They were hoping to get us in there so they could pull off a raid on the aircraft.

Still, nobody came forward with the answers to my two simple questions.

About the time we were ready to begin our descent into Beirut,

I made contact with Tel Aviv and asked the agent there if he could help me with the same two questions.

I was feeling very frustrated, because I was just broadcasting blind, telling whoever was out there what was going on, how many hijackers there were, how they were armed, and so on. I would have felt better if some trained antiterrorist expert had come on to receive my information and comment on my requests. But I never talked to anyone like that. Instead, I talked to air traffic controllers and ticket agents.

While I was waiting for Tel Aviv to get back to me, I happened to see, out of the corner of my eye, Jihad reenter the cockpit. Sitting down in the seat behind me, he took a pair of headphones and slipped them on. I knew then that the jig was up. Quietly, and as subtly as possible, I reached over and switched the radio off-frequency so Tel Aviv could not get back to me.

If we were going to stop this continual flying back and forth, and if we were going to avoid flying into a potentially much worse situation in Tehran, we had to do something soon.

Jihad stepped out, I looked over at Christian, and he gave me a slight, imperceptible nod. We both knew, if we were going to do something, it was now or never.

The Nightmare Drags On!

"Ohmigosh! Look at that!"

Christian pointed at a rather insignificant gauge on the instrument panel.

"Something's wrong here! We could be in big trouble!"

"What is it?" I leaned over to get a look at it myself. A couple of our "hosts" were right behind us, worried looks on their faces.

Christian kept ranting about the big trouble we were in, and Phil and I joined the act.

I had learned in Algiers that Phil was a masterful actor, but he didn't have anything on Christian. Listening to him go on and on about what bad shape our engines were in was scaring me, and I was in on the act!

On this trip from Algiers to Beirut, we had spent as much time as we could talking about ways to stop the flying. It really wasn't

95

safe to be doing all of this flying without having any maintenance done on the aircraft. I had insisted on a quick preflight in Algiers, but aside from that we had flown thousands of miles with no maintenance checks. It was also true that this continuous flying was wearing the crew down. We were exhausted, and it was not good to be flying in that condition.

If we couldn't come up with a way to stop it, they would probably keep us flying back and forth until the airplane fell apart, or until we finally ditched it into the Mediterranean.

"Guys," I had said, "We have to figure out some way to stop this flying! Let's work on it."

Christian suggested that on our next landing we could run off the end of the runway. Phil thought perhaps we should hit the brakes at high speed, thereby blowing all the tires. Most of the ideas involved dramatic clouds of smoke and dust and caused me to shift uncomfortably in my seat as I thought of them.

We had even talked about ditching in the sea, just offshore, but then quickly dismissed the thought.

As we were discussing that particular idea, I had thought to myself, *Man, we're supposed to be able to do a belly landing in the water with one of these things, but nobody is an expert at that sort of thing. The books says you can do it, but I'm not too sure the book knows what it's talking about! It's all theory.*

Finally, I said to Christian, "Why don't we just see if we can fake a couple of engine failures. That way, in case we have a chance to escape, we'll have something to escape in."

And now, Christian was pulling off our "engine failures" with a masterful job of acting.

Suddenly, he pointed to another gauge.

"Oh, no! Here goes another one!"

"Hold on!" I yelled. "I think we can make it!"

We were already headed into the Beirut airport, and if we played it just right, we'd "lose" the engines just about the time we were rolling to a stop.

As we touched down, Christian reached over and closed the

fuel valve to engine number two, and the engine began to spin down toward idle.

Not only did he close the fuel valve, but he also reached over and switched his electrical bus selector to that engine as well. Then as the engine ran down, the generator ran down, too, and this touched off a display of flashing lights, which made it look like big-time trouble.

"Oh, oh!" I said. "There goes two!"

Meanwhile, Christian had reached over and done the same thing with engine number three. By the time we had rolled to a stop, that engine, too, was gone.

I shoved up the throttle on engine number one, and we slowly moved off the runway. When we were safely parked, I turned that engine off, and we just sat there. I turned to Jihad and shrugged my shoulders.

"These engines were way overdue for an overhaul," I said. "They're gone. There's nothing more we can do."

He pointed his finger at me. "Now listen! Don't you kid me about this! This is not a good place for you to be!"

"We know that," Phil said.

"Yeah," Christian added, "they don't like Americans here."

"If there was any way we could start it up, we would," I said. "But man, it's gone! You saw what happened!"

He thought for a minute and then came up with a solution.

"No problem! We'll get a mechanic from Middle East Airlines to fix!"

"No," I said, "that won't work! You saw what these engines did. They're gone—past repair."

"Oh. Okay . . . Middle East has engines."

"That's a good idea, but it won't work either. They have 707 engines and this is a 727. They won't fit."

"Oh," he slumped down in his seat, chin in hand, trying to think of another solution.

I shook my head and sighed. "There's nothing we can do but

bring in new engines from the states. And that will take at least two or three weeks."

He nodded his head in disgust. But if there was nothing more we could do, that's all there was to it.

The primary reason we were able to pull off such a stunt was that the hijackers were, by this time, beginning to trust us. We had cooperated with them on everything they had asked us to do, and I believe they had begun to think of us as their friends. They were not stupid people . . . and it certainly would have been harder to convince them of our engine failures if they had not come to trust us.

We sat where we were all that afternoon, while the hijackers had discussions with the control tower. At one point, another hostage, Bob Peel, Sr., was released because he was ill.

Later that day, they dropped the rear stairs down, and several more heavily armed men came on board. This began a continuous switching of the guard. For the next sixteen days, we would remain aboard the airplane, while dozens of guards came and went. They seemed to have a regular schedule worked out, and I remember at one point one of them telling us that he was happy because the next day was going to be his "day off," and he would get to see his family.

As evening fell, word came that an Israeli gunboat was cruising just offshore, and armored vehicles were near us firing at it. This made our captors nervous, and they wanted the plane moved to a more sheltered spot. We shared that feeling so we started up engine number one and slowly moved the plane around to the other side of the airport.

Later that night, sometime around 1:30 or 2:00 A.M., more members of the militia arrived. They went through the aircraft, waking everybody up and telling all of the passengers to get ready to leave the plane.

We didn't know what was going on and couldn't get any answers from anyone. But within half an hour or so, everybody had left the plane except Christian, Phil, and me, and, of course, our guards.

A short time later, a group of militiamen came back to the plane and asked us how they could get into the belly of the aircraft.

Up until this time they had been content to go through the luggage kept in the overhead bins and hadn't said a word about the luggage stored in the plane's cargo compartments. They probably didn't even know there were such compartments.

I suspect that one of the passengers must have tipped them off while leaving the plane, when he said something like, "Hey! What about my luggage?"

"What luggage?"

"My bags in the cargo compartment."

"Aha!"

When they asked us how to get in the plane's belly, we feigned ignorance.

"We don't know anything about that," I said. "We just fly the thing, we don't know how to get in there."

"I think it's pretty hard to do," Phil lied.

It wasn't. Even without our assistance, they were in there in a matter of minutes. With the back stairs lowered, they began dragging mailbags and suitcases up into the cabin. After that their procedure was exactly the same as it had been with the overhead bins.

They rummaged through suitcase after suitcase, taking what they wanted and dumping the rest onto the floor. When one suitcase was empty, they would throw it on the floor and start on the next one. The cabin had been a mess already, but now I was beginning to think we would drown in the debris. There were business papers everywhere, mixed in with bottles of whisky, underwear, and souvenirs. The plane was beginning to look like the aftermath of a bad tornado!

When the sun first peeked over the Lebanese horizon that day, I had to think back to the beginning of our ordeal to figure out what day it was. It was Monday, June 17, day four of the hijacking, and two days away from my wedding anniversary. Two days away from what was supposed to be a leisurely cruise among the Greek islands with my wife. I wondered about her, where she was and what was going on in her life. I prayed that she was okay and able to cope with all of this. I knew that wherever she was, she was praying for me, and I drew strength from that.

Being held hostage was terrible for many reasons, but for me one of the worst was not knowing where my wife was or how she was coping—and it was especially hard at the time of our anniversary.

That morning, we got the first answers about what had happened to the passengers. They were safe, we were told, and had been taken to various houses throughout Beirut.

That didn't sound promising. If they had been taken to different houses throughout the city, that meant it would be easier to maintain control over them—it also meant that someone might be planning on this situation dragging on for some time to come. I kept thinking about what had happened in Iran a few years earlier, when American hostages were held for 444 days. The people who had kidnapped us looked to the Ayatollah as their spiritual inspiration. Could it be that they would seek to emulate him in this instance? If that were the case, we could be here for a long, long time.

Around ten that morning, they brought us our first Lebanese breakfast . . . and it was delicious!

It started off with Lebanese bread, which is round and thin, very much like Mexican tortillas. It came in big, thick stacks. Then there were containers of ripe, black olives and more containers of unflavored yogurt mixed with olive oil.

And there were cheeses—lots of cheeses. I discovered that my favorite way of eating was to take some yogurt and olive oil and spread it on a piece of the bread. Then I would put a few chunks of cheese in there, fold it over, and it made a very good sandwich. In the meantime, I would be dipping into a container of olives.

It wasn't exactly the sort of breakfast one gets used to on a farm in Missouri, but it was good all the same.

It was about this time that the terrorists must have decided they wanted to impress us with their hospitality.

"Captain, more food?"

"Oh, no! I'm full!"

"Here, you take . . . you like!"

If it wasn't bread or cheese they were pushing at me, it was orange drink. We were practically swimming in orange drink, and we couldn't drink enough of it to make them happy.

Then one of the guys, a fellow we later came to call Fat Ali, found something that he was sure I would like better.

"Hey, Captain," he called out, "whisky!" He held up a fifth of Cutty Sark.

"Yeah, whisky," I agreed.

"You want?"

I shook my head. "No, I don't want it."

He looked shocked and brought the bottle over to me. Perhaps I hadn't heard him right.

"You American," he said, trying to hand the bottle to me. "American like whisky!"

"No . . . not this American." I pointed to my chest.

"But . . . all Americans like whisky!"

"No, all Americans *don't* like whisky."

He couldn't believe it. He wandered off, shaking his head, to see if either Phil or Christian wanted the whisky. Neither did. I suspected these people had picked up their ideas about America from watching old gangster movies.

Throughout our "vacation" in Beirut, we often came up against the idea that all Americans like to drink, that crime is rampant in the United States, and that we are, in fact, a nation of gangsters.

One of the hijackers harped constantly on the theme that America is a decadent place, and that all we do over here is hang around in discos and behave shamefully. He was so convinced of that fact that we took to calling him Disco Ali.

It became somewhat of a challenge to us to uphold our country's honor, and to show our hosts that we were every bit as moral as they were. At the same time, we were all extremely grateful that their religion would not allow them to touch alcoholic beverages. They were very well armed, at all times, with guns everywhere, and it could have caused some serious problems if any of them had had too much to drink.

We felt better after our breakfast, although having some food in my stomach made me realize what a pitiful sight I must be. I hadn't shaved in four days, and my beard was at that itchy, scratchy point where it feels like you're beginning to turn into a porcupine. I hadn't been able to take a bath, or change my clothes, and I wasn't feeling very elegant.

It didn't help, either, when I looked at Christian and Phil. They both looked like refugees from the nearest gutter, and I knew that I didn't look any better than they did. That hurt.

This overwhelming feeling of "dirtiness" was compounded by the trashiness of our surroundings. Trash from the passengers' suitcases was everywhere, scattered up and down the aisles, literally two-feet deep in some places. The cabin looked like the nightmare of every mother with teenage children: a total, absolute mess!

Other than the mess in the cabin and our unwashed state, we were relatively comfortable. We were running the auxiliary power unit, which allowed us to keep the air conditioner on, and it felt good not to be worried about flying off to Algiers, or Aden, or Tehran.

Still, it would be nice to get a shower and perhaps put on some clean clothes. I asked one of the guards if we could possibly go somewhere and freshen up.

He replied with a noncommital, "We see."

But in the meantime, they had another treat for us: newspapers.

There was the *Beirut Daily Star*, the *International Herald Tribune*, and a *USA Today*. These three newspapers were brought to us on a regular basis—not every day, but particularly when there were articles about us or photographs of the airplane, which was frequently.

And, almost every time they brought us the papers, they would encourage us that, "It's good! You go home! Maybe tomorrow!" Or they would excitedly tell us, "Two more days! Then you go home!"

They weren't trying to mislead us. They were almost as anxious as we were to get this thing over with. They wanted to get their own people back, and I honestly believe they wanted us to be reunited with our loved ones. We learned very early in the ball game, though, not to get excited when they started talking about our imminent release.

But on that first Monday morning, we were especially delighted to get the newspapers because, for the first time, we were able to find out what was really going on. Up until then, we had heard that the hijackers were demanding the release of prisoners held by Israel, but we had no idea who these prisoners were, or even if they really existed. Furthermore, we didn't know anything about the political situation in Lebanon. We knew there was a war going on, but we didn't know what it was about, nor who was fighting whom.

From the newspapers, we were able to understand the current situation in Lebanon. The *Beirut Daily Star*, in particular, had a number of excellent articles that presented an entire overview of the events that had led up to our hijacking.

We learned that Israel had moved into Lebanon to strike against the Palestine Liberation Organization, which was using its bases there to launch terrorist raids against Israel.

It seemed that the people of Southern Lebanon, by and large, did not care for the PLO occupation of their land and welcomed Israel's move across their border. But in time, Israel's harsh, ironfisted policy and her reluctance to pull back across the border had deeply angered the Lebanese people, who felt they had exchanged one occupying force for another.

Israel had ultimately withdrawn from Lebanon, but in the process they had taken over seven hundred Lebanese hostages to secure the safety of the departing troops. The hostages were supposed to have been released when the withdrawal was complete, but instead were moved across the border into northern Israel shortly before our hijacking and held at Atlit prison camp.

Hijacking our plane was an attempt to gain the release of those prisoners through American pressure on Israel.

We also read that Nabih Berri, who is Lebanon's justice minister as well as the leader of the Amal militia, had assumed responsibility for negotiating our release. Berri was quoted as saying he was in a very difficult situation, walking a tightrope. On the opposite side of the issue, President Reagan was saying that Berri could end the ordeal anytime he chose.

There were various quotes from Israeli officials, more quotes from President Reagan and members of his cabinet—and, all-in-all, it did not look as though we would be going home any time soon. It was a very complicated situation we found ourselves in, and we didn't know the proper solution. All we knew was that we wanted to go home—and we thought those Lebanese citizens sitting in the Israeli prison camp probably felt the same way.

We also discovered the subtle division of responsibilities between the Amal and the Hisbollah. The Amal, it seemed, had taken charge of all the passengers who had been removed from the aircraft. We, on the other hand, were still under the control of the Hisbollah party. The Hisbollah wanted control of the aircraft as a symbol of their role in this affair.

This gave us a somewhat better understanding of the difficult position Nabih Berri found himself in. He had to negotiate a solution that would please both the more-moderate Amal and the extremist Hisbollah. If he didn't come up with something that pleased both groups, he would most likely become another casualty of the Lebanese civil war!

Reading the newspapers was definitely the high point of that first full day on the ground in Beirut. The rest of the day we sat in our seats, napped off and on when we could, and quietly talked or read books. I mentioned to the guards a couple of times that something should be done about all the trash and asked again if we might go somewhere to clean up, and they told me that something might possibly be arranged. But I was given no assurances.

In the meantime, I noticed that our tough, anti-American guards were smoking constantly—Marlboros from America—and that they would flip their butts onto the floor, right on top of all the trash littered there. (I thought it was interesting that, despite all their anti-American rhetoric, they smoked American cigarettes, drank American soft drinks, especially Pepsi, and many of them wore T-shirts with the names of other American-made products printed on them.)

I told anybody who would listen that it wasn't safe to be throwing cigarette butts on the carpet like that and that they had better get all that stuff out of there before the whole plane went up in flames.

Finally, they decided that maybe I knew what I was talking about. Monday evening, we were taken off the plane and walked across the ramp to a nearby firehouse, where we sat on the patio with our guards and watched cleanup crews remove the trash from the airplane.

They worked for hours, pushing all the trash out the back end of the airplane—only it wasn't really trash. It was business papers, credit cards, family photos, souvenirs, clothes, colognes, and other items that had been important to the passengers on TWA Flight 847.

As they pushed all of this out the back of the aircraft, crews were waiting on the ground below to shovel it into trash bags—and they filled dozens of bags. They started shoveling around midnight, and it was 3:00 A.M. when the job was finished.

As trash bags were filled, they were taken to the side of the firehouse and tossed into a huge bonfire blazing near where we were sitting.

Among all of the items being burned were numerous bottles of liquor, and there was a continuing series of explosions as the fire found them.

"It figures," Phil said, after one particularly violent explosion.
"What figures?" I asked.

"Well, we've survived the hand grenades and having guns pointed at us all the time. So now we'll probably be killed by an exploding bottle of Jim Beam!"

We laughed. But not long after he said that, the entire countryside was lit up by an eerie bright light.

Was that a whisky bottle? We looked around and saw a magnesium parachute flare descending over the nearby hills.

The flare was followed by several exchanges of machine gun tracer fire, another flare, and more gunfire. Then everything faded back to silent darkness.

The guards paid no attention whatever, but it was a reminder to us that we were being held in a war zone—that Beirut is a divided city, and battles were raging all around us. The most frightening thing about it, to me, was the nonchalance with which it was accepted, as if war and killing were a normal part of day-to-day life.

It was also at the firehouse that we first became acquainted with some members of the regular Amal militia, and they impressed me because they were much better educated and less fanatical than the Hisbollah. We were able to engage in gentle debate with them, and they appeared willing, at least, to listen to our point of view. They did not come at us continually with wild pro-Khomeini statements.

On board the aircraft, our guards would want to tell us all the time about the greatness of the Ayatollah, and they never tired of talking about the evils of America. But if you showed the slightest indication of winning debating points, they would quickly change the subject and attack from a different direction. They had been fed their hate propaganda, and it served the useful purpose of transferring blame for the mess they were in from their own shoulders to remote, alien America. Any other point of view was rejected.

As for these Amal, there was no doubt at all that we were on opposite sides of a great many issues, but it was good to find people who at least were interested in dialogue.

About two in the morning, as we were sitting on the firehouse patio, I happened to look over toward the airplane. Two of the inflatable emergency slides were visible, deployed from the rear emergency doors. Someone had come up with the idea of opening those doors, and when he did, the slides automatically went into action.

"Oh, brother!" I shook my head, and told one of the guards we would have to go over and take a look at the plane. It wasn't a major problem, and yet it made me wonder how much damage would be inflicted on the aircraft by our "hosts." They didn't understand the plane and didn't seem to respect her. I began to think that perhaps we should try to find a way to convince our guards that we couldn't stay on board the airplane much longer.

We unfastened the two slides and let them fall to the concrete runway below. Then we deflated them, rolled them up, and stuffed them into the cargo bay. One of the guards was right behind us, asking if he could have one of them for a souvenir.

He probably wanted to inflate it and use it for a raft. I had visions of him bobbing along on a Beirut beach, bragging to anyone who would listen about his part in the hijacking of TWA Flight 847.

He was disappointed when I told him he couldn't have it, but he didn't argue with me.

"Listen," I said, "those things cost an awful lot of money, and they are an integral part of the aircraft.

"An airplane can't fly without them, and I just can't let you have one."

No more was said about it that night, although I doubt if those slides ever made it back to the United States.

When our time at the firehouse was through, it was good to see that the airplane's cabin was almost back to normal. There didn't seem to be any lasting damage to the royal blue carpeting, and the seats were in pretty good condition, except for a few places where they had been used for bayonet practice! The only other evidence of the hijacking was the graffiti that had been scrawled everywhere, but mostly on the doors of the overhead bins, in red Magic Marker. Most of the graffiti was scribbled in Arabic, but here and there were messages in English.

Reagan we not afraid you was one message that stood out. And, of course, there were a few of the *Death-to-America* type and some words of praise for the Ayatollah.

But all in all, things looked pretty good.

Unfortunately, they didn't stay that way for long. The guards were clean personally, but they couldn't learn not to throw their trash on the floor and didn't seem to have the slightest concept of normal housekeeping.

Probably the trash-on-the-floor routine was part of their macho, tough-guy self-image. At home, they had wives or mothers who picked up after them. They were the warriors, and warriors didn't have time to worry about picking up after themselves. After living with these men for a few days, I must say I developed a high degree of sympathy for the wives and mothers who picked up after them!

Every morning, I would go into the cockpit to see what kind of a mess had been made overnight. I would find a thick stack of half-eaten bread sitting on the engineer's table. Empty Pepsi cans were always strewn all over the floor, along with cigarette butts and mounds of bread crumbs. There were also plenty of shell casings, where several rounds of ammunition had been fired off for some reason or another—usually to get the attention of the tower.

They were always shooting their guns, and that was something we adjusted to fairly quickly. During our time of captivity, the gunfire was constant.

One day in particular, we thought the plane must be under

attack from outside sources. One of the guards ran into the rear of the plane, lowered the back stairs, and began firing off bursts from his AK47. At the same time, two other guys were blazing away from the cockpit. Blam! Bloom! Blam! It sounded as if World War III had erupted. And then they were running back and forth, thundering up and down the aisle. They'd fire a few rounds from the back, then squeeze off a few more from the front, and they kept it up for quite a while.

I grabbed one of them as he ran past.

"What's going on?"

He jerked his arm away from me and ran on past without answering.

I raised my window shade and looked out to see if I could learn what was causing all this commotion. All I saw was a Middle East Airlines jet, sitting on the ramp across from us, loading passengers. They were no more than a few hundred yards away from all the gunfire, but were paying no attention whatsoever! From the way they were reacting, you would have thought they were in, say, Albuquerque on a peaceful morning, not here in Beirut with gunfire blazing all around them.

Eventually, the gunfire died down and as I continued looking out the window I saw one of the Follow-Me jeeps heading our way. A few minutes later, one of our guards came running into the cabin with a huge bag full of sandwiches, and the Follow-Me jeep drove away.

The guard began handing out sandwiches, so I figured whatever the emergency had been, it was over.

As soon as I could, I stopped another of the guards.

"What in the world was all the shooting about?"

He looked embarrassed.

"They said they weren't going to bring us any sandwiches."

So that's what it had been. World War III over the airport's refusal to bring sandwiches!

The next day the *Beirut Daily Star* had a dramatic article describing how the hijackers had launched an all-out attack on the press. What had really happened was that the reporters and photographers had congregated on the second-floor balconies of the terminal, because that gave them a good view of everything going on below. And those balconies just happened to be in the direction of the gunfire. When the terrorists started firing, the members of the press corps hit the deck.

The *Daily Star* described in exciting detail how the bullets had ricocheted off the terminal building and how the reporters and photographers had gone scrambling for their lives. It was amusing to read that story and know that the whole incident actually took place because the terrorists wanted a bag of sandwiches.

But as for the messes in the cockpit, it eventually got to the point where the entire floor was an unsightly, crunchy, nauseating mess, made up of equal parts of crumbs, cigarette ashes and butts, and spilled cola.

It was hard for me to accept this, because the airline always makes such a point of keeping the cockpit area clean—especially for safety reasons. Pilots are reminded constantly not to set any liquid—coffee, juice, or whatever—on the radio console. It's a good rule, because one spilled drink could ruin the radios.

But these guys would sit in the two pilots' seats, with the radio console between them, and eat, drink, and smoke all night long, sloshing their drinks and spilling crumbs down into the radio.

One morning it was a particularly bad mess.

"Look at this place." I said.

No response.

"This place looks like a pigpen!" I scolded. "Do you people know what pigs are?"

One of the hijackers slowly rose to his feet, sighing as he wiped crumbs from his shirt and pants.

"Yes," he said. "We know what pigs are."

"Well, I don't know how you can live like pigs!"

I snatched up a trash bag and began picking up as much of the mess as I could.

They seemed to respect me as the captain of the airplane, and if I could pick up trash, perhaps they could too—at least this once.

They made no secret of the fact that they weren't happy about it, but the two men who had been on overnight guard duty in the cockpit took trash bags and helped me pick up some of the mess. We continued to pick up trash in the days following and noticed the guards beginning to follow our example. The cabin environment began to improve somewhat, but most of the mess on the cockpit floor was untouchable. The sun pouring through the windows had hardened it into an ugly, smelly sort of concrete, and it would take a professional cleaning crew—or perhaps dynamite—to get it up.

Two months later, when a TWA crew went into Beirut to fly the airplane out, they found out just how bad it was. They told me the radio console was covered with green mold, and that when they tried to tune the radio so they could talk to the tower, the tuning knob broke off in their hands. They had to be very careful with the other radio, too, they said, because they could barely tune it.

When they attempted to turn on the automatic pilot, they couldn't budge the large toggle switches; they were frozen in position.

What the guards didn't throw on the floor or let fall into the radio console, they just tossed out the cockpit window. After we had been aboard the plane for several days, there was a large pile of garbage on the ground around the cockpit.

Another problem was that they did not understand or appreciate Western-style bathrooms. Specifically, they didn't know how to use the toilets. They were accustomed to Arab-style squat toilets and would stand up on the toilet seats instead of sitting down on them.

And they splashed water instead of using toilet paper. They brought Evian bottled water aboard by the case and put most of it in the lavatories. Then, for their sanitary purposes they would splash water on themselves. Of course, most of the water cascaded down onto the lavatory floors and out into the aisles. It didn't take long before the carpeting around all three lavatories was completely soaked and squished when you walked on it.

The hijackers would walk across those wet carpets on their way into the lavatories and then stand up on the toilet seats with their wet, greasy shoes. The floors in the lavatories were flooded, and the sinks were a revolting mess.

After a few days of this, I pulled aside one of the guards who spoke fairly good English and negotiated with him.

"We come from different cultures, and we do things differently in our lavatories," I told him. "How about if we keep one of the lavatories just for us, and you keep the other two?"

That sounded reasonable to him, so he got a Magic Marker and wrote something in Arabic on one of the lavatory doors. For the rest of our stay in Beirut, the hijackers respected the fact that that was "our" lavatory. We kept it military neat and clean, and I began doing my laundry in the sink.

But if I wasn't nagging the hijackers about picking up their trash, I had to keep telling them to leave the equipment alone. They were like kids with a new toy—constantly flipping switches and pushing buttons just to see what would happen.

Whenever I would catch them I would reprimand them:

"You don't know what you're doing, and you shouldn't touch these controls!" I felt that as captain of the aircraft, it was my responsibility to keep it in the best condition possible, hijackers or no hijackers.

I would talk to them like a father might when he had to discipline his teenage sons, and they generally responded. Most of our guards were young men, barely out of their teens, and they regarded me as the old grandfather, so they would usually listen when I told them not to do something or other.

But no sooner would I get one group to stop flipping switches than it would be time for a changing of the guard, and a whole new group would come on board. Then the new arrivals would discover the same things I had told the others not to do. It was a never-ending battle.

There was no doubt that their two favorite toys were the radio and the public address system. If they weren't talking to the tower for hours on end, they would most likely be barking orders or serenading us over the P.A. system.

I rarely went into the cockpit without finding someone talking to the tower. They would take my uniform coat out of the closet, sit in my seat, and have a great time pretending to be the pilot talking to the tower. In time, they were clearing aircraft for take-off or landing.

By then, they had given all of us nicknames, and we had returned the favor. I was "Captain Abu Ali," Phil was "Abu Ahmed," and Christian they called "Abu Muhammad." They got particular pleasure out of changing Christian's name to Muhammad, one indication to me that our hijackers, as serious as they were about their cause, were not without a sense of humor.

We gave the guards nicknames, too, primarily because we couldn't keep their real names straight. Most of them were named either Abu or Ali, and if you called out either one of those names, at least half a dozen of them would have responded.

"Captain Abu Ali! Captain Abu Ali!" My name would be called out over the P.A. system.

I'd put down my Bible or my newspaper and head for the cockpit. What did they want this time?

"Captain Abu Ali, you tune radio?"

"Okay."

They would talk on the radio so much that they were tying up the tower's frequencies. Finally, the controllers would ask them to switch to another frequency because they were interfering with traffic. Only they didn't know how to change the frequency, so they'd have to ask me to do it.

But talking on the radio wasn't nearly as bad as serenading us over the public address system. The first time I heard one of them crooning a mournful, wailing, Arabic song, I thought we must be under attack. But it was three in the morning!

For some reason, they especially loved to sing at night, like wolves howling at the moon—only wolves are more musical. I don't know if it was the songs themselves or merely the way they sang them. But I have a feeling it was probably both, and it made for a devastating combination.

After a couple of nights of this, I knew something had to be done.

I called a powwow with Christian and Phil.

"Listen, guys," I told them, "we have to do something about these midnight serenades!"

"Oh, yeah," Phil agreed. "I don't think I can take any more."

"We're going to have to find a way to disable the P.A. system," Christian agreed.

We decided to look for the first opportunity to disable the system. It was the only way we'd get a decent night's sleep.

Later that afternoon, we got our chance. I sauntered into the cockpit as if I was out for a leisurely stroll—just stretching my legs. Three of the hijackers were sitting there, gulping down Pepsi, their loaded guns beside them.

I sidled over to the wall and put my shoulder up next to the circuit breaker for the public address system. Once I was in position, it was an easy matter to reach up and "scratch" my shoulder, flipping the circuit breaker to the "off" position at the same time.

Nobody paid any attention at all. I yawned, turned, and strolled out of the cockpit, then I sat back down in my area of the cabin and began reading a book.

It was nearly two hours before they noticed that the system was "broken." Then one of them came to me with a very worried expression on his face.

"Captain Abu Ali, radio broke!"

"No kidding?" I tried to look surprised.

"Yeah, won't work!"

"Okay, I'll come have a look at it." I put my book down and followed him into the cockpit, where two of the other guards were tapping on the microphone.

"Let me see that," I said. I took it in my hand, tapped it a few times, blew into it, and then set it back in its cradle.

"Yep, you're right. It's broken."

One of them looked at me hopefully. "You fix?" he asked.

"No, I can't," I said. "You guys broke it. You talked on it too much."

I shrugged to say there was nothing more I could do. Then I turned and walked out of the cockpit, leaving them tapping and blowing into the microphone, hoping that somehow it would come back to life.

That pattern continued throughout our captivity. We were constantly looking for ways to shut systems down. If they were doing something that was potentially damaging, we'd discuss ways we could stop it. If what they were doing wasn't harmful or particularly annoying, we'd let them go ahead. But I had never before seen people get so much pleasure out of flipping switches, pulling levers, and punching buttons. And there wasn't a button on the aircraft that they didn't push.

One morning, I came into the cockpit to find the fuel-dump switch door open. This is the first part of the procedure that allows you to dump fuel if you run into an emergency. I looked out under both wings, and there was no fuel on the ground. Okay, I thought, at least they hadn't opened the tank dump valve. I reclosed the door and told them to leave that door and those fuel-dump switches alone.

A few days later, we were running low on fuel because of our continuous use of the auxiliary power unit.

I fired up our one "good" engine, and we taxied over to the refueling area to take on another load of kerosene. But as the truck arrived and started pumping the kerosene, it immediately began cascading out the right wing dumpchute.

We stopped the fueling, and I opened and closed the fuel-dump switch a few times. Then we tried it again. No luck. Again, the fuel came pouring out onto the ground.

We repeated the procedure several more times, without luck. For some reason, the dump valve was stuck in the open position, and we couldn't get it closed.

We called some mechanics from Middle East Airlines, and they came to see if they could help us solve the problem. We came up with several ideas, but none of them worked.

"I don't know," I said. "If we can't get that valve closed somehow, we can't put fuel on board, and if we can't do that, we can't run the APU. And if we can't run the APU, we can't have our air conditioning . . . so we'll have to leave the plane and go somewhere else."

The guard who would later appear at the cockpit window with us during our TV interview was standing nearby and heard this with pleasure.

"Oh, good!" he enthused. "Now we can blow it up!"

He pulled a hand grenade off his belt, walked over to the cargo area, and made ready to toss the grenade into the cargo bay. He seemed almost giddy, as if a jet airliner exploding into flames was something he had always wanted to see.

"Cool it! Cool it!" I yelled at him. "We'll get the thing fixed!"

He shrugged his shoulders, fastened the grenade back onto his belt, and let out a sigh of disappointment.

At the same time, another guard was walking under the wing. For some reason, he reached up with the butt of his AK47 automatic rifle and gave the underside of the wing a vicious whack.

There was an immediate response: a slight purring sound, as the motor-driven valve ran closed.

I looked at the mechanics, who stood there with sheepish grins on their faces. Why hadn't we thought of that? It's the oldest trick in the book. Everybody knows that when something won't work, the best thing to do is to give it a good thump or two!

"Try it again!" I called to the truck driver.

This time, it worked fine.

The following day, the *Beirut Daily Star* carried a photograph of me standing outside the airplane with my arm around one of the terrorists. The caption said something about the two of us having a "friendly chat."

What had really happened was that I was trying to make myself understood above the roar of the auxiliary power unit. I had been trying to talk to the hijacker about our attempts to get the valve closed—and in order to do that I had put my arm around his shoulder and shouted into his ear. At that exact moment, the news photographer snapped the photo. From the photo, you would have thought the hijacker and I were old buddies, out for a stroll. Hardly.

Not long after that, I was sitting back in the cabin, trying to write a letter to Phyllis, when the whole airplane began to shake up and down. I stopped writing and listened. It didn't sound as if the wind was blowing that hard, and I didn't hear another airplane blasting past us.

I went into the cockpit to see what was going on. There, I found my answer. One of the guards was sitting in my seat. He was holding the yoke and jerking it back and forth, full travel, continuously. With three thousand pounds of hydraulic pressure supplying the muscle, the heavy elevator high atop the tail was lurching up and down, up and down—and the entire aircraft was shaking violently as a result.

I told him to stop, and he did. But when it came time for a shift change, one of the new men discovered the same game, so I deactivated the elevator power.

Another day we were standing in the aisle talking, when we heard a strange swishing noise overhead. This was a weird sound, and certainly nothing I had ever heard before.

I looked at Phil. "You ever heard anything like that before?"
"Not me."

Christian sighed. "I wonder what they're doing this time."

The three of us went forward to the cockpit, where we found our answer. This time, the guard sitting in the captain's seat was listening to music through the earphones of his tape player and tapping both feet on the rudder pedals. The rudder was bouncing back and forth to a rock 'n' roll beat, and we were hearing the control cables in their runs back through the cabin structure.

The guards were fascinated with the cockpit and had immediately moved in as soon as we had shut down and climbed out of the pilots' seats. Since we had spent more than enough time in there already, we were happy to go back into the now-empty cabin and set up housekeeping there. We chose seats in the coach cabin near the overwing exits, wherever we could find a relatively clean spot. That Tuesday was a quiet day spent sleeping, eating, and establishing our "hovels," as Christian called them. My bed was seats 15 A, B, and C, with row 14 seatbacks folded over as needed for dining table, footrests, or what have you. As night was falling, Jihad came to me with some concern and said that we would have to move the airplane to the backside of the airport. He would not say why, but the location was away from the sea, behind some remote hangars.

I imagine they had gotten fresh reports of a possible Israeli commando attack from the sea and wanted to hide the airplane. So we started up our one "good" engine and began to move the aircraft.

It was dark by this time and hard to see where we were headed. Some of the landing lights had burned out; in fact, all I had left was one light, which was in close to the fuselage on the left side of the aircraft. That didn't really help me too much, and it was necessary to weave back and forth in order to see ahead.

As I was taxiing down this dark, deserted part of the airport, I had to keep maneuvering around big piles of concrete blocks and structural steel. They were apparently using this as a staging area for construction work that was going on around the airport, and there were some dicey moments as Phil, leaning out his open window, would call out, "Here's a big one on my side!"

Boy! I thought. *If my chief pilot could see what I'm doing with his airplane, he'd fire me in a second!*

Finally, we made it the three-quarters of a mile to our new location, shut down the engine, and parked the plane.

"Okay," the leader told me, "this is fine."

So the three of us went back to the cabin to lie down and try to get some sleep. But we hadn't been back there for more than twenty minutes when he came back again.

"Got to move the airplane."

He wouldn't tell us what had happened, but something back there on that dark, deserted side of the airport had caused them to be extremely nervous.

So, we had to start her up again and make our way back through the obstacle course, until we finally parked exactly where we had been parked before.

The longer we were on board, the more convinced I became that we had to find a way to get off the airplane before the hijackers did some serious, irreparable damage. There was no guarantee that our stay in Beirut was going to be a short one, and the aircraft would not hold up if our captivity stretched into weeks—or months.

I was also afraid that the auxiliary power unit would not hold up, because it is not designed for long-term use. Christian, Phil, and I discussed the issue, and we finally decided that the best thing to do was to fake a failure of the APU, just as we had with the main engines.

A failure of the APU would serve two purposes: One, it would prevent the terrorists from continuing to wear down the airplane's electrical and mechanical equipment. Two, it would serve to get us off the aircraft and perhaps into safer, more comfortable surroundings.

As I lay in my makeshift bed that night, I tried to think of ways we could shut down the APU and get off the aircraft.

But as was usually the case, my thoughts wound up drifting to Phyllis. Again, I wondered where she was, what she was doing, and I said a prayer that she was okay and able to handle all of this.

I knew that she had a deep faith in God that would comfort

and sustain her. And yet I also knew that the hijacking had come at the worst possible time. There could be no good time for something like this to happen . . . but the next day was our wedding anniversary—and it would be an especially difficult one for both of us.

"Lord," I breathed, "please just do something to let her know that I'm okay and how very much I love her."

6

Phyllis's Story

When I walked back into my empty, lonely hotel room on the evening of our anniversary, there, waiting for me was the biggest, most beautiful bouquet of flowers I had ever seen. The card said they were from John, and that he loved me and missed me on our anniversary.

I had been fighting back the tears all day, and when I saw those flowers and read the card, the floodgates opened. It was almost more than I could bear, and yet, seeing the flowers and reading that card were reminders, not only of John's love for me and mine for him, but of the fact that God was watching over us and keeping us both in His care.

The flowers were not really from John, of course. He had no way to send flowers, or even a "hello." But friends of mine—I called them my support group—had joined me in

Athens to watch and wait for John's release; they had sent the flowers for John.

The first few days after the hijacking, I kept up hope that the ordeal wouldn't last that long. Surely John would be set free and come flying back into Athens, and I wanted to be there when he did. But as the days crawled by, I became less sure of the outcome and more uncertain about whether I should remain in Greece, return to the United States, or just what I should do.

The morning John had left on his flight to Rome I was excited and happy because we were going to have that wonderful anniversary cruise among the Greek islands. That was something we had talked about and looked forward to for a long time. When John's fellow pilot Sean Shattuck called me that first afternoon, I was still absentmindedly thinking about the romantic trip to come. It didn't really register when he said, "I guess you haven't heard about the hijacking."

"What hijacking?" I asked, not thinking for even one second he could be talking about John.

"Oh, I'm sorry, Phyllis . . . I thought you knew."

Suddenly, he had my undivided attention. My heart was racing and my throat became dry.

"Knew what?"

There was a pause on the other end of the line. Captain Shattuck hadn't wanted to break the news to me in this way. But now he had no choice.

"I heard about it on television. John's been hijacked."

"Oh, no! It can't be!"

We talked for a few more minutes, but I don't remember what else was said.

When I finally hung up, I just sat there for a few minutes, staring out the window, past the terrace where John and I had eaten our romantic breakfast just a very few hours earlier. I tried to pray but had no idea what to say.

122

"Jesus. . . . Jesus. . . ," I kept repeating His name over and over. It wasn't much of a prayer, but I knew that He heard my desperate cry for help.

Later on, when I had a chance to talk to Captain Shattuck again, he told me that he had been surprised by my strength.

"You asked me some very intelligent questions," he told me.

"I did?"

"You did. I thought I was dealing with an emotional giant!"

"I hate to admit this," I said, "but after you said John had been hijacked, I don't remember anything else at all."

The few days after the hijacking were an absolute horror for me. I cannot describe the anguish I felt when I heard the news that one of the plane's passengers had been murdered.

How could human beings treat other human beings this way? I didn't care what the hijackers' "cause" was, and whether it was just or not. Nothing in the world gave them the right to shoot down innocent people in cold blood. And, of course, after the killing occurred, I knew that John was in the hands of monsters, and even though I believed the situation was in God's hands, I was afraid of the possibility that he might not be coming home to me at all. And, too, I kept thinking about Iran, and the 444 days American hostages were held there. What would I do if John were held captive that long?

The first twenty-four hours after the hijacking were especially hard for me because I didn't know anyone in Athens. The phone rang constantly—in fact, I received more than two hundred calls that first day, mostly from friends and relatives who wanted me to know they loved us and were praying for us. Those calls helped, but I needed personal contact—a shoulder or two to cry on.

Those shoulders came in the form of my friend Marie Sendelbach, who flew from Chicago to be with me. I also received much needed strength and support from two other dear women, Judy Baker and Carol Bergeron, who had come to Athens to be with their husbands, who are also employees of TWA. When they arrived in Greece, though, they discovered that their husbands had left the country, on special assignment for the airline. What none of us knew was that they had gone to Cyprus to work with a Delta Force type of rescue team.

Two other members of my support group were Captain Shattuck and TWA Director of Flying, Captain Clark Billie, who watched over me and protected me, especially from the prying eyes of the press.

Reporters were constantly trying to get to me during those days in Athens. Although I now realize they were just doing their jobs, at that time I was in no condition at all to talk to them. After a while, in fact, I began to regard them as nothing more than vicious wolves, who would not leave me alone in my time of sorrow. Some of them went to great lengths to have a few words with me, and I found their aggressiveness frightening. Couldn't they understand that I wanted to be left alone?

If it weren't for my support group, and the Lord, I never would have made it through those days.

I didn't spend a lot of time in prayer, as strange as that might sound from someone who was counting on the Lord's intervention and protection. The truth is, I couldn't pray. I just didn't know what to say. I did take comfort in the biblical truth that God knows what we need before we even ask Him, and He knew the heaviness of my heart, and I considered the attitude of my heart to be a form of prayer. Plus, I was receiving hundreds of supportive messages from friends and relatives who told me they were praying for us, so I knew they were praying the prayers that I myself could not pray.

I did spend a great deal of time reading the Bible, especially looking for promises of God's protection and care. As I read,

I would write down the verses that seemed to speak most directly to John's situation.

One of my favorites was Deuteronomy 31:6: "Be strong and of a good courage, fear not, nor be afraid of them: for the Lord thy God, he it is that doth go with thee; he will not fail thee, nor forsake thee."

Those words seemed to leap off the page. I knew as I wrote them down that God was speaking directly to me. I called our pastor, Brian Guy, back in Missouri, and told him that the Lord had given me that verse of Scripture as a particular comfort and promise. That night, unbeknownst to me, Brian led the members of our church in a prayer meeting, which centered around the theme of that special Scripture. Over the next several days I would read those words over and over, dozens of times, finding comfort in them each time.

When our anniversary arrived, my support group took it upon themselves to lift my spirits.

"Phyllis," Marie told me, "you are not going to sit around your room all day. You have to get outside."

She said it gently, but firmly, and I knew she was right.

So Marie, Judy, Carol, and I walked down to the hotel's marina and spent most of the morning just watching the boats going out and coming in. As much as I attempted to join in the conversation and be a part of things, I wasn't going anywhere without my portable radio. I kept it tuned to Armed Forces Radio and kept a plug in my ear all morning, hoping to hear the news that would really make this an anniversary to remember: the news that John and the other hostages were on their way back home. But, of course, it didn't come.

The only good news was that the airplane had been sitting on the ground in Beirut for two full days now. It didn't look as though they were going to be flying anywhere else. That was a relief to me, because while they had been flying back and forth, I had been absolutely frantic.

After our morning at the marina, we had lunch together,

and I was advised that I was going to be their guest of honor at an anniversary dinner that night. They were as sweet and as kind to me as they could be—but I think I could have handled it better if they had been rude and thoughtless! For some reason, kindness was just about the hardest thing in the world for me to take, and as the day went on, the aching emptiness deep inside my chest grew worse and worse, and it became harder and harder to hold back the tears.

The dinner that night was even more difficult. The ladies were joined by Captains Billie, Shattuck, and McIntyre, and all of them were trying to be optimistic and lighthearted for my sake:

"I hear that negotiations are going very well."

"Yeah . . . he'll be back home in a day or two."

"Seems like a lot of progress is being made."

But all the optimistic talk in the world wasn't going to help me that night—especially when the orchestra kept playing those heart-tugging romantic melodies, and the man I love was being held at gunpoint by a group of radical outlaws, who had already demonstrated their willingness to commit murder.

Finally, I excused myself from the group, telling them that I was sorry, but I thought it would be best if I went back to the room. As I looked around at all of their faces, I could see the sadness they really felt, the sadness they had been trying to hide on my account. I appreciated their concern and told them so. But I hoped they would understand that I just needed to be alone. They did, and nobody tried to stop me.

"We just want you to know we love you," Marie called out, as I left the table. I didn't turn around to acknowledge her words. I couldn't.

When I got back to my room, I found the flowers waiting for me, and that's when the dam broke. I must have sobbed for an hour, maybe more.

When I got to the point where there wasn't another tear

within me, I picked up the telephone and called Brian again. We talked for a while and then prayed together, and that made me feel better—not good, but better.

If only I could have more assurance that things were going to work out.

A short time later, the telephone rang. It was John's daughter Diane, calling from Missouri:

"Everything is going to be good! I saw Dad!"

"What do you mean you saw him?"

"He was on TV, and he looks great! Everything's going to be okay!"

After I hung up the phone, I breathed a quiet prayer of thanks. That was the best news I had received in a long, long time. John wasn't any closer to freedom. But I knew now that he was all right—and that was the second-best news I could hear!

Above: The fifty-dollar airplane as purchased.

Top left: John and his Harley-Davidson.

Top right: The young aircraft mechanic tuning up a new Ercoupe in Tulsa, 1950.

Right: The new pilot with fiancée, Pat Humphrey, and the freshly restored PT-19.

Above and right: Flight Engineer Testrake and his first "large" aircraft, a PBY Catalina Flying Boat, at Whidbey Island, Washington. He was assigned to this navy patrol bomber from 1950 to 1953.

Below: Capt. Bob Wilson, Pan Am, and Capt. John Testrake, TWA, at annual get-together in Oshkosh, Wisconsin. The aircraft, a Fairchild PT-19, is identical to the one they bought, restored, and flew together in 1950-51. *Inset:* Bob and John — best friends, fellow students, and budding aviators at Spartan School of Aeronautics, Tulsa, 1949.

Capt. Testrake and hijacker at cockpit-window news conference, June 19, 1985.

Above: One of the hijackers points his pistol toward an ABC American television crew from the cockpit window.

Right: One day before the release of their hostages, June 29, some of the hijackers are shown waving to photographers.

Below: On June 20, the hijackers themselves took some photos. Here Capt. Testrake is shown in the cockpit with two hooded hijackers.

Above: The crew of Flight 847 at an awards luncheon given by TWA in New York.
Back row, left to right: Flight attendants Judy Cox, Helen Sheahan, Elizabeth Howes,
Hazel Hesp, and Purser Uli Derickson. *Front row:* Flight Engineer B. Christian
Zimmermann, Capt. Testrake, and First Officer Philip Maresca.

Below: Phil Maresca shows his famous spider bite to newsmen at a New York press
conference on July 3, 1985. Capt. Testrake is wearing uniform retrieved from the
hijackers; First Officer Maresca and Flight Engineer Zimmermann are wearing
uniforms provided by Middle East Airlines pilots.

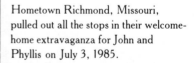

Hometown Richmond, Missouri, pulled out all the stops in their welcome-home extravaganza for John and Phyllis on July 3, 1985.

The parade car was almost lost in the Main Street crowd upon its arrival in town.
Escorts included State Highway Patrol from Kansas City Airport to the county line,
Ray County Sheriff to the city limits, and Richmond police to the Courthouse Square.
Note friends and newsmen atop buildings.

Left: Capt. Testrake at home with the Bible he carried during the hijacking.

Left: John and Phyllis with Pastor Brian Guy at the Christian Fellowship Ministries Church in Richmond.

Above: Capt. Testrake and grandson Patrick Smith in the cockpit of the hijacked airliner on a happier occasion—its return to Kansas City from Beirut in August 1985.

Right: John and Phyllis arrive in London in September 1985 to receive a special medal struck by the Guild of Air Pilots and Air Navigators.

7

Days Into Weeks

Wednesday morning in Beirut. Day six of the hijacking was shaping up as another warm, lazy day, and there wasn't much news in the morning papers. It looked like the hijacking was getting to be an old story, and the reporters were already digging hard to come up with new things to write about it.

Suddenly, one of the many terrorists we knew as Ali came charging into the cabin, waving his gun around, and saying something about reporters.

"What?" I put down the newspaper. "Slow down and tell us what you're talking about."

"We are having a press conference," he explained. "Reporters are coming out this morning, and you will talk to them!"

"Where? When?" We were all asking the same questions.

It seemed that our captors had arranged for a group of newspaper and television reporters to come to the airplane. They would stand on the ground outside while we would be allowed to answer their questions from one of the cockpit windows. The reporters would be from the French news agency, Agence France Presse, or from ABC News. Other news-gathering organizations would not be represented.

Ali was extremely excited about the press conference—probably because he saw it as his big opportunity, his moment in the sun. He would be able to flash his gun around in front of the entire world, and all, of course, in behalf of "the cause."

Ali's father was a wealthy merchant in Beirut, which meant he was well educated and spoke nearly flawless English. For that reason, we had a better relationship with him than with some of the others, although we never knew what he would come up with next. He would be friendly and helpful one minute, and then, in his next breath, he'd talk about how great it would be to blow up the plane.

At one point, he had come up with the idea of flying the plane to Jerusalem and crashing it into the Knesset while the Israeli parliament was in session.

When he made that suggestion, I laughed and acted as if I thought he was kidding. But it was sort of a nervous laugh, because I knew he *wasn't* kidding! Whenever one of them came up with an idea like that, you didn't want to take it too seriously, because if you did, you were afraid that might spur them on.

Ali had given up, at least temporarily, his idea of crashing into the Knesset, but now he had something almost as exciting to occupy his time. He would be the "moderator" of our press conference. That meant he would get to hold his gun to our heads while we answered questions, he would decide when the press conference was over, and he would also be able to fire a few shots at any reporters who got too close to the aircraft.

It was mid-morning by the time he finally ushered us into the cockpit. Several other hijackers were waiting for us, and they, too, seemed to be especially excited about all the attention they were getting.

A small group of reporters had already gathered outside the airplane. There were television cameras, still photographers, and a few reporters with notebooks and tape recorders.

Ali opened the "press conference" by leaning out of the cockpit window and showing his gun, making it known that reporters who didn't toe the line would be in big trouble. He was also showing off and immensely enjoying his moment in the limelight.

He didn't seem to want to relinquish the stage.

"Okay, that's enough!" I cracked. "Come on back in here."

He pulled back inside the cockpit and motioned for me to take my place in the window. I introduced myself to the reporters and began answering their questions.

"Captain Testrake," someone asked, "what has happened to you and what is happening now?"

"Not very much is happening to us now since Sunday night," I answered, "because they removed the other passengers and took them away, and the three of us have been on the aircraft since then. It's just a case of wait and see what happens . . . so we've just been doing housekeeping in the aircraft."

Behind me, Ali was still trying to get into the act. First he would look out the window to see what was going on, then he would point his gun at my head. The reporters must have thought I was in immediate danger of being shot if I said or did anything wrong. I didn't think that was the case, because I had a fairly decent relationship with Ali. But still, with these people you never knew what was going to happen, and so I tried to measure my words carefully.

"Are you well treated?" came another question.

"Yes."

"Are you able to eat what you want to eat?"

"Well," I laughed, "they sometimes bring us airline food and they sometimes bring us Lebanese food—and it's different to us but it's very delicious. I'd say on the whole the food is okay."

"Can you talk to them?" someone wanted to know. "Do they speak English? Can you communicate with them?"

"Sometimes better than others. It depends on who's on board."

I was asked if I had any idea what had happened to the passengers who had been removed from the plane. I didn't, except that I had been told they were safe and comfortable. Someone else asked if I had any messages for my family. I was grateful for the chance to answer that, although I wasn't sure exactly what I was going to say.

"Yes," I responded. "I would like for my wife and my family and all of my friends back in Missouri to know that the Lord has taken very good care of us so far. He's seen us through some very trying times, and He'll see us through to the end."

One final question. I was asked whether I was in favor of anyone launching a rescue operation.

"I think we would all be dead men if they did, because we're continually surrounded by many, many guards."

I hoped that statement would be heard clearly, especially by the people associated with the Delta Force.

Now it was Ali's turn to get back in the act. He reached around, put his gun in front of my face, and then pulled me back away from the window with his other hand. My part of the press conference had come to an abrupt end.

Phil was up next in our "window television," and he told the reporters that his message to his family was that "They can worry a little but not too much. Our treatment has been tolerable."

Following Phil, Christian made a brief appearance. He sent greetings to his family, including his eighty-eight-year-old father, telling them that everything was okay, and "we're surviving."

Christian didn't know that his father, the Reverend Elmer Zimmermann, had died of a heart attack a few days previously, while attending a prayer vigil for his son.

Christian also got a brief chance to mention that the Lord was watching over us, but by this time, the hijackers were nervous and jumpy.

Christian was pulled back into the cockpit, just as a man with a camera was spotted trying to get close to the back steps of the plane.

"Trick! Journalist!" someone yelled. Then there was a loud burst of automatic weapons fire.

Apparently, a reporter had tried to trick the hijackers by driving up to the plane in a food truck. He got out of the truck, acting as if he were making a food delivery to the plane. But then someone saw his camera, and that's when everything broke loose. The press conference ended amidst a flurry of gunfire and shouts to confiscate the man's film.

I didn't know why the hijackers had called the reporters to the plane in the first place, but I assumed it was another attempt to show the American and Israeli governments that they were serious about their demands. They probably also wanted to show off the fact that we were getting along fairly well and not in any desperate situation. I guess they thought that might help them in their negotiations.

Whatever their reasons were, I was delighted that we had had a chance to communicate to the outside world. I was especially glad that Phyllis would finally be able to hear from me, even though indirectly.

It was after the press conference that the media first picked up on the fact that Christian and I are both Christians. The next day, as I read the news reports about our press conference, I discovered that our statements about the Lord's care were prominently mentioned. For the first time, I began to realize that something good could come out of this mess. When people saw how the Lord was sustaining Christian and me during our time of trouble, perhaps they would be encouraged to turn their lives over to Him, as we had.

And it was true that every single moment of the hijacking, no matter what was going on or what threats were being made, I felt very strongly that the Lord was with us—and if that were true it didn't matter who was against us.

Besides allowing us to get messages to our families, the press conference also gave us the chance to do something we had been trying to figure out how to do: shut down the auxiliary power unit.

When the unit is operating it makes a loud noise, and there was no way we could talk to the reporters over its roar. The first request the reporters made of us was "Would you please turn off that loud machine?" We were happy to oblige.

I looked over at Christian and gave him a little wink.

"Sure. We can turn it off!"

I gave Christian a hand signal, he pulled the switch, and the unit purred to a stop.

We were delighted to turn it off because it had already been running continuously for nearly seventy-two hours, and I had never heard of one running that long. They are just not made for that kind of usage. The APU is a miniature gas turbine engine, the same as the main thrust engines, except smaller. It's used for air conditioning and electrical power until the main engines are started, and for other intermittent uses.

We wanted to shut it down for two reasons: one, because we knew it was not good for it to be on all the time, and two, because if we shut it down, our hosts would have to move us off the plane. No one could take being cooped up in a tin can without air conditioning during a Beirut June. Getting off the plane would make sure that it incurred no further damage, and it would also do us good to get into more comfortable surroundings, where we might be able to do things like take showers and shave more often.

As soon as the press conference was over, we were ordered to turn the air conditioning back on. It had already become stifling aboard the aircraft, in just the few minutes the APU had been off.

Christian flipped the switch to the "on" position. Nothing happened. He looked worried.

"Hey, something's wrong here. It won't come back on!"

"Oh, brother!" I pounded my fist into my palm. "I knew we were running it too long!"

Christian and I struggled valiantly for a few minutes to figure out what was wrong, but without luck. Of course, we both knew that the real cure was quite simple: just turn the circuit breaker on.

We broke the bad news to Ali. Without the auxiliary power unit, there would be no air conditioning. Not only that, but the radio wouldn't work, and there would be no communication with the tower. But the thing that really got to them was the fact that without the APU, the hydraulic pump that was used to raise and lower the back stairs wouldn't work.

That was important. They always came onto the plane through those back stairs. Then, as soon as they were safely inside, all they had to do was push a lever and the stairs would come up and lock snugly into place. When the stairs were locked up they felt safe in their cocoon, but when the stairs were down they were exposed and vulnerable, especially to a raid by the Israelis, which they were always expecting.

"Isn't there another way to get those stairs up?" one of the English-speaking guards asked.

"Well, yeah," I answered. "There is a hand pump."

"Christian, why don't you go back there and show them how the hand pump works."

The hand pump is on the outside of the aircraft. You open an access panel, pull out a telescoping lever, and then you pump, and pump, and pump. When you reach the point where you think you just can't pump anymore, the stairs may or may not latch closed.

I watched from the cockpit window as several of the men pumped the stairs into position while Christian supervised. It took a while, but after several minutes of huffing and puffing underneath the bright sun, the stairs were up and locked into place.

Naturally, I wanted to make sure they had it right, so I hit the release button. The stairs unlocked—and came tumbling back to the ground.

"Okay!" I called out. "Try it one more time."

But Ali wasn't having any more of it.

"This is no good!" he yelled. "Even if we used the pump, someone would be left out here."

One of the other guards muttered something in Arabic.

"Yes, and it's too slow!" Ali fumed.

They came back in and talked back and forth for a while, trying to decide their next move. Finally, one of them made a decision. They would bring in mechanics from Middle East Airlines to fix the APU, so I knew they were determined to have it.

"Well," I said, "why don't you let us take another look at it. Maybe we can fix it."

So that's exactly what we did, and we made a big production out of it.

Christian got out his flight engineer's technical handbook, and we opened it at random to a wiring diagram of a wash water pump, or something similar. We studied that for quite a while, pretending that we were trying to fit together the pieces of some terribly complicated puzzle. It was a silly game, but it was a nice break from our usual routine, and we were having fun.

I would say, "You know, I think it's probably the right-hand relay that controls the frammis."

Christian would agree. "You're probably right. If only we can figure out the proper angle on that frammis!"

Finally, we decided that the "problem" lay just behind a particular access panel, so Christian took the cover off.

He peered in for a moment.

"Nah," he shook his head. "It's too dark in here. I can't see a thing!"

One of the guards was right there, offering him a flashlight.

He looked in with the flashlight, while I continued to study the diagram.

"Oh, yeah!" he said. "I see it! There are three contacts on the top, and two on the bottom."

I looked at my diagram. "Yeah, that's it."

And then, step by step, we went through the repair of an imaginary piece of equipment.

We, too, were relieved to get the APU back on, because the air conditioning felt really good! We hadn't succeeded with our plan to get off the plane, but we had some fun, and that was good for us.

Incidentally, for the next two weeks, the APU continued running without a hitch, and it was still going strong when we were finally set free. Christian kept oil for it in the overhead bin above his seat and checked its oil level frequently.

The next day, Thursday, passed pretty much without incident. There were no major breakthroughs in the negotiations and not much other news.

Then, that evening about eight-thirty, we were told that we would be going to the terminal for a press conference at nine.

"Hey, I don't know," I said, when they told us about the press conference. "I'll have to check my social calendar!"

Nobody smiled. Either they didn't get it, or they didn't think it was funny.

But then nine o'clock rolled around and nothing happened.

"What time are we going to the press conference?" Phil asked.

"Well . . . there's a problem. Later."

We waited a few more minutes. Still no word about the press conference.

Then, about nine-twenty, a terse announcement was made: "No press conference!"

That was fine with me, because I really didn't like being put on display. I was beginning to feel like the prize catch in a fishing contest, and I resented it.

We found out later that the press conference had been canceled when a near-riot broke out among the reporters gathering at the terminal. What had begun as a carefully orchestrated press

137

conference had erupted into a mob scene. Five of the other hostages had been present to answer questions, but when things didn't go as the hijackers wanted, the rest of the evening's "program" was canceled.

They were indignant, of course; they didn't understand why the members of the media couldn't behave in a more civilized fashion!

They didn't get much sympathy from me, because I figured if they, themselves, were civilized, they'd let us go home to our wives and families.

I didn't think we needed another press conference anyway, because there was nothing new to report.

But, of course, every day when the newspapers arrived, I would grab one and look to see if anything had happened overnight.

Friday morning was no exception, and I was looking at a copy of *USA Today*, which featured an account of our Wednesday-morning press conference. There, on the front page, was a photograph of Zimmermann, speaking from the cockpit window. The cutline underneath the photo mentioned that Christian had sent greetings to his father, as he was unaware that his father had passed away several days earlier.

I looked across the aisle. Christian was, as usual, silently reading his Bible. I watched him for a minute, wondering how to tell him that his father was gone. But I knew there was no good way to give news like that and figured I might as well get it over with.

I went over and stood beside him while he read.

"Christian?"

He stopped reading and looked up. "Hey, John. Come on in and sit down."

"Listen," I said. "I have something to tell you, and. . . ." I paused, not knowing how to say it. Christian just looked at me, without saying anything.

I went on, "It's about your father. I was reading the newspaper"—I sat down beside him—"and it says that your father has passed away."

Christian still didn't say anything; he just nodded his head.

I handed him the newspaper and showed him what I had been reading. After he had a chance to read it, we sat together in silence for another minute or so.

Finally he said, "I wish I could have been with him. But I know he's gone home."

He went on to tell me that his father had served God for many years, and that he was a man full of faith and the love of Christ. He had lived a full life, including many years of missionary service in China, and Christian knew it was time for him to go to his eternal home.

"It makes it easier, too, knowing that I'll see him again some-day. Thanks, John."

When the guards found out that Christian's father had died, they were extremely apologetic. They were very family oriented and they sympathized with him greatly over the loss of his father. But he always gave them the same reply: He knew his father was in heaven, and he would be able to see him again someday. I'm not sure they fully understood what Christian was saying, and I know they were more than a little surprised that he did not carry on with weeping and wailing, which would have been their style.

To me, this was just another example of their unpredictable nature. They kept telling Christian how sorry they were that his father had died, and yet there was very little remorse expressed over the death of Robbie Stethem. We felt sure that the guards who were now holding us would not have killed Stethem. That was the work of the original two hijackers, and we had no idea what had happened to those two.

On at least two occasions, I tried to talk to guards about Stethem's death and what a senseless tragedy it was. And every time, they would bring up the *New Jersey*.

At first, I didn't know what they were talking about. In fact, during the time when we were still flying back and forth between Algiers and Beirut, one of the terrorists went running up and down the aisles of the plane yelling, "New Jersey! New Jersey! New Jersey!"

I couldn't understand it.

"What has he got against New Jersey?" I asked. "It's not my favorite place either, but why is this guy so violent about it?"

But in our later discussions, I found out that the reference was to the battleship that had bombarded Beirut after terrorist attacks on our marines there killed more than two hundred young men. Whenever I brought up the brutal murder of Stethem, the guards would rapidly shoot back horror stories about the shelling by the *New Jersey.* They referred to the 2,700-pound shells as flying Volkswagens.

Almost every one of them had a friend or a family member who had died in that shelling. I wondered if the *New Jersey* was what had convinced some of them to join the Hisbollah militia.

One guard cried as he told me that he had lost every single member of his family during the *New Jersey* bombardment. He told of not knowing what to do or where to run while the explosions sounded all around him.

They made it very clear that they held President Reagan personally responsible. They had nothing against the American people, they assured me, but they considered our government to be totally evil.

I didn't really remember much about the bombardment of Beirut. I recalled the bombing of the marine barracks and my anger and sorrow over the loss of so many young lives. But I began to wonder if we had retaliated in a proper fashion.

I spent a lot of time thinking about it. Could we find a way to hit back at terrorism without hurting innocent people? Were we justified in firing indiscriminately into a city where many thousands of innocent people live—people who just happen to be caught in a war they don't want?

Of course, nothing we had done could justify the killing of Robbie Stethem. But I was beginning to understand some of their anger and see that they, too, had suffered for things they had not done.

I was thinking about all this on Friday afternoon, trying to sort it out and make some sense of it, when something started happening.

First of all, the guards started acting extremely nervous and excited. Then, all of the other guards started pouring into the plane, twenty-five or thirty of them perhaps, as if they all had been called back to active duty. They were always heavily armed, but this was ridiculous. They had enough ammunition to stave off the Israeli army—and I wondered if maybe that was what they were going to have to do.

Then they all started taking pillows out of the overhead bins. They yanked off the pillowcases, began cutting eyeholes in them, and pulled them over their heads. In a matter of minutes, it looked as if we were being held hostage by a group of trick-or-treaters.

"What's going on?" I asked Disco Ali.

He turned and ran off without a reply.

"What is it?" I demanded of Abu. He wouldn't tell me either.

I watched out the window, as they all hit the ground, lying in prone position, like infantrymen, all around the aircraft. There was no doubt that they believed we were under attack of some kind. But by who? I didn't have the slightest idea.

In spite of the pillowcases, I recognized one of them as Jihad. He climbed up on a loading platform, which was on the back of a pickup truck. I could see that he had something in his hand that wasn't a weapon. It was one of our bullhorns. But then the truck began moving away from the aircraft, and I couldn't tell what was going on.

There were some shouts and loud noises, but strangely enough, no shooting.

It wasn't until the next day, when we read accounts of the incident in the *Beirut Daily Star*, that we learned what had happened:

It seems that a mob made up of anti-American demonstrators

had whipped themselves into a frenzy. They wanted to show their dislike for America and decided the best way to do it was to burn the airplane. Whether we would have been allowed out first wasn't clear.

The mob had already reached the airport when our captors sprang into action, in a valiant effort to "head 'em off at the pass." I don't know what was said through the bullhorn, but it worked. The mob apparently burned an American flag, yelled a few insults about the United States being in league with Satan, and then they went home.

Phil, Christian, and I found it ironic that the men who were holding us against our will had been forced to assume the role of our protectors. But we knew they were more interested in protecting the airplane than they were us. The plane was their prize. They were proud of the fact that they had captured it and they weren't going to let a bunch of strangers come in and take it away from them. Besides, if anyone was going to destroy the airplane, it was going to be them!

We got a chuckle out of an editorial in the *Daily Star*, which described how everyone in Beirut was threatened on a daily basis by the war raging throughout the city. The newspaper said that the only ones who didn't have to worry about it were those of us who were being held hostage in the city. We were dubbed "the best protected" people in all of Beirut.

And I suppose it was true. We *were* a lot safer inside than we would have been outside. As a matter of fact, we had ample opportunity to escape, but didn't try for several reasons—one of which was that there was a war going on out there, and we had no idea where to go.

The guards had grown so lax in their treatment of us that there were times when we probably could have walked off the rear end of the plane or gone out the wing exits. And we plotted doing just that.

We knew that Israeli picketboats were riding offshore, but they were five miles or more out, and that's a pretty long swim through

142

shark-infested waters. We talked about walking north along the beach until we reached Turkey, or south to Israel, but we didn't really think either idea was practical.

We considered seeking asylum from the Middle East Airlines people on the field. But in a sense, they were as much hostages as we were, and we felt it would cause them embarrassment and trouble to ask them for help they could not give.

Another thing we had to consider was that we were not the only hostages. If we were able to escape, what would happen to the others? We didn't know—and didn't want to take chances with their lives.

We knew, too, that there were negotiations going on, and any attempt at an escape would surely delay an agreement.

There was also the matter of the airplane. We felt responsible for this ship and didn't want to just abandon it.

But still, despite all of those reasons not to try an escape, it was a constant source of speculation and temptation.

This was especially true because the hijackers were always leaving their guns lying around. I couldn't make up my mind if they were really that careless, or if they were just tempting us to see what we would do.

We would have had fairly easy access to guns and ammunition, but there wasn't any valid reason to try some sort of Rambo stunt. We didn't even know how to release the safeties on the Russian guns, as compared with the hijackers' lightning-fast handling of their weapons. It was also plain that they would have shot us down instantly had we tried a firefight.

The first few days after we were on the ground in Beirut, they had been more careful with their guns. But then on the third or fourth day, they brought in a big feast of Lebanese food. There was fried chicken, olives and cheeses, and all sorts of strange and wonderful things. I had no idea what they were . . . but they were delicious. They folded down some seatbacks, which they used for a table, and then folded down several more for us to sit on.

We sat cross-legged and helped ourselves to the big circle of food in front of us. About halfway through the meal, I happened to look back at the folded-down seat just behind me, and there was somebody's AK47 assault rifle. I was sitting on somebody's gun!

When we finished eating, and most of the guards had left, the gun remained stuck down in the seat. Pretty soon, one of the guards came wandering back through the cabin with a forlorn look on his face.

"I lost my gun." He said it in the tone of voice you might expect from a little boy looking for a lost dog.

"Oh," I told him, "it's right behind that seat over there."

When he saw it, he let out a loud sigh of relief.

"Thank you," he breathed, clutching his gun to his chest.

"You're welcome!"

Their careless behavior was probably created in part by their casual attitude toward firearms. These young men had been around guns all their lives. That was obvious by the way they played with them. I would watch them jack the bolts open and closed, take the ammo clips on and off, and so on.

I heard reports that prior to our final landing in Beirut, some of the hijackers were forcing the passengers to play Russian roulette. If that's true, there is certainly no excuse for frightening people that way. But I watched them playing games with their guns enough to know one thing: If they didn't want a gun to go off, it wasn't going to. At no time, despite all the guns and ammunition on board the aircraft, was I ever afraid that someone might be shot accidentally.

It wasn't accidents I was worried about. It was the guards with the hot tempers who concerned me.

One of them in particular was absolutely devoted in his allegiance to Ayatollah Khomeini. He kept a photograph of the ayatollah, which he flashed around the way an American youngster might an autographed photo of George Brett or Joe Montana.

He pushed Khomeini to the point where you would have thought he was on the ayatollah's payroll.

One day, I had had enough.

"You like Khomeini?" he asked me, again.

"No!" I exclaimed, giving him a double thumbs-down. "Khomeini is bad!"

He looked at me as if he knew he hadn't heard me right. "What?"

"Khomeini is bad. He kills his own people!"

I didn't know what kind of response that would get, but I figured it wouldn't be a very good one.

Instead, his eyes widened as if he realized that I had hit upon some new truth. He didn't say anything more, but just walked away. We hadn't heard the last about the wonders of the ayatollah, but we were at least spared for a little while.

Another thing I was worried about while we were being held captive was my weight. You can put on weight pretty fast when you're just sitting around—and that's about all we were doing. We'd eat, read a while, take a nap, eat again, take another nap, eat some more, and then it would be time for bed!

And the food came on board in great abundance. There would be perhaps nine of us on the plane—six hijackers and the three crew members—and they would call the tower and demand seventy-five sandwiches. They never seemed to be satisfied that we had had enough to eat.

They were young men who seemed to operate on the same principle as sharks. In other words, they could eat all the time.

"Captain Abu Ali, another sandwich?"

"Oh, no thanks." I'd pat my stomach. "I'm full."

"Here! Another sandwich," and one would be thrust into my hands. I couldn't stop them from giving me food, but I couldn't possibly eat or drink everything they brought me, and so I would set it aside, thinking I'd look for an opportunity later to dispose of it. After a while, I accumulated quite a stockpile, especially of cartons of orange drink. Sometimes I felt as though we were awash in a sea of orange drink. There seemed to be an endless supply of the stuff.

Once in a while, our guards would make a special effort and bring us something they knew we liked—hamburgers and french fries. I don't know where they came from, but they were good, and it was nice to be eating "American food." The rest of the time, when the menu didn't consist of cheeses, olives, and Lebanese bread, the food was supplied by Middle East Airlines.

The guards would open one of the windows, fire off a volley of shots, and pretty soon someone would bring fifty or sixty little casserole dishes on board. When we saw those dishes, we always knew we were going to have chicken—usually a drumstick and a thigh always covered with a tasty tomato sauce. Actually it wasn't half bad, even if we did do a lot of joking about having to eat airline food all the time.

We never stopped being amazed at how much food our captors could put away. We never could understand where they were putting it all, but we assumed they wanted to get it while they could. They probably figured that once we were released, the gravy train would stop. As long as they had us, they had an unlimited expense account, and they were making the most of it!

They were young enough that they didn't have to worry so much about putting on weight. That wasn't true of the rest of us. We needed a great deal more exercise than we were getting.

One day I asked Phil if he wanted to do something about it.

"What do you say we get a little drill going here?" I asked him.

"Fine!"

So we stood up at the rear of the cabin and began marching in close-order drill up and down the aisle of the plane.

"Hup! Two! Three! Four!"

Now, one thing I'd learned very early in the hijacking was not to sleep with my legs sticking out into the aisle. The guards would go running up and down the aisle at all hours, so having your legs sticking out was dangerous—especially during the middle of the night when the cabin was dark. I almost had my legs broken a couple of times before I found another way to sleep.

But as Phil and I marched up and down the cabin, several of the hijackers were sleeping with their legs extended into the aisle. Tough luck, guys! We decided it was their problem. We were getting some exercise and that was that.

"Hup! Two! Three! Four!" Stomp! Stomp! Stomp! Stomp!

We'd thunder down the aisle one way, watching several pairs of legs being pulled in to avoid a collision. Then we'd do a military about-face and march back down the other way, watching the legs pull in again, like turtles withdrawing into their shells.

I'm sure the guards thought we had totally lost our minds, but we continued to march for about an hour, enjoying ourselves and acting like a couple of kids. A jetliner cabin is not a bad prison cell—plenty of seating and thirty-three paces long.

It was strange that all the time we were marching, the rear door of the aircraft was open, and the stairs were down. Every time we marched to the rear of the cabin, we were heading right toward that open door and the freedom that lay beyond it. It would have been so easy for us to just keep marching, right off the plane and onto the ramp below.

We didn't say anything, but I was thinking about it, and I know Phil was, too. Even though our hearts might have told us to go for it, our heads told us we couldn't. We figured that we might have a fighting chance to reach freedom, but we didn't want to risk messing things up for all the other hostages. So we didn't try to make a break.

All during this time, I was doing my best to keep a log of everything that was going on—using the backs of business letters and other papers that had been strewn around the cabin by the hijackers.

One afternoon, I looked up from my writing to see one of the guards hovering over me, a curious look on his face.

"What you writing?"

"It's a business letter."

Without a word, he snatched it out of my hand and stalked off. I figured he probably couldn't read English, and even if he could, I hadn't been writing anything that would get me into terrible trouble. Still, I expected to hear some more about it and perhaps be told to stop keeping a log, but nothing ever happened.

I hated to lose it, because so much was happening so fast that I wanted to keep a current record, and now I would have to rely on memory to reconstruct those first few days.

However, a few days later while walking in the aisle, my eye fell upon a familiar-looking paper half buried in the debris, and I bent down to pick it up. It was my missing manuscript, and I still have it—rumpled and covered with hijackers' bootprints.

Then one morning several days later, I was writing my thoughts about the murder of Robbie Stethem and musing about some of the violent mood swings I had encountered in the hijackers.

"Captain Abu Ali! Captain Abu Ali!" came blaring over the public address system. I was wanted in the cockpit for some reason, probably to change the frequency of the radio again. I set my writing aside, got up, and went into the cockpit, where I took care of whatever it was they wanted.

But when I came back into the cabin, my heart skipped a beat or two, because my log was in the hands of a new guard—a man I had never seen before. He was a hard, mean-looking sort. He had bushy eyebrows and thick spectacles perched on his nose. Everything about him seemed to say *troublemaker!*

He looked at me suspiciously and held up the paper in his right hand. "What is this?"

"Give me that!" I snatched it out of his hand. "That's a letter to my wife." I lied. "You go ask Ali. I write to my wife every day."

I folded the paper, slipped it into my shirt pocket, and dropped angrily into my seat.

My opponent shrugged his shoulders, turned, and headed for the cockpit. He was going to do as I suggested: ask Ali about my letter-writing habits. Fortunately, it was true that I wrote Phyllis every day, and most of the old-timers knew it.

In a few minutes, he was back to tell me in halting English that he wanted to apologize. He was sorry for looking at the letter.

"Well . . . that's okay," I grumbled. "But this is personal!" I patted my pocket.

"I am sorry."

"It's okay!" We shook hands and he wandered off. But I didn't start working on the log again right away. It took an hour or so for my hands to stop shaking and my heart to climb down out of my throat.

I also breathed a silent prayer of thanks that the hijackers were so family oriented. They cared deeply about their wives and children, so they understood that it was difficult for me to be separated from my family. They allowed me privacy in my communications with Phyllis and offered to send them out with Middle East Airlines crews.

If there was one thing the hijackers liked to talk about, besides Khomeini, it was their families. One day one man was positively giddy because he had earned a few days off and was going to be able to spend some time with his wife and two children. Others would tell us about their wives and children, or their parents, and when they did, you could see the hard edges melting away and a wistful look in their eyes. Those were the times when I felt most strongly that, in spite of the situation we found ourselves in, we were all brothers in the family of man.

What a tragedy that the world has divided into armed camps, where men and women are killed just because they are Americans or Jews or Arabs. I don't mean to get on a soapbox or be melodramatic, but when you sit down with your enemy, and he starts telling you with love and pride in his eyes that his baby daughter is learning how to walk, it does something to break down the walls and make you realize that all men are created in the image of God. Even if we do fall far short of what we're meant to be.

As our captivity entered its second week, life on the plane was becoming routine. We all had our schedules worked out, and except for the boredom, the separation from our loved ones, and the unpredictable mood swings of our captors, life was moving along at a normal pace.

By this time I was doing my laundry in the little sink in our lavatory, and I was shaving every day. I was also taking "baths" with a washcloth and doing my best to stay clean. But still, a shower was a tremendous luxury, and I was always happy on the rare occasions when we were granted a visit to the firehouse for that purpose.

Those few occasions always came in the middle of the night and were usually as brief as possible. We'd shave, shower, eat a bite or two, and then head back to the airplane.

But one night, for some reason, our hosts were in a particularly generous mood.

When we were finished with the showers, someone asked us, "How would you like to sleep at the firehouse tonight?"

Would we! We were like a bunch of excited kids whose father had just told them they would be allowed to "camp out" in the backyard tonight!

We were taken to the patio, where a big spread of refreshments had been prepared. There were several juicy, ripe watermelons, sweet red cherries, biscuits, tea, and assorted other goodies.

It was a beautiful summer night, and the velvet sky was ablaze with what seemed to be a million stars. If the circumstances had been different, it would have been an altogether enjoyable experience.

Christian and I decided we would sleep outside, under the starry sky, which spoke to us so eloquently of God's creative hand—and reminded us that He was with us in every situation. Two army cots were brought out for us, and we slept very comfortably. Phil, on the other hand, opted to sleep inside, in the barracks that was used by the militia troops.

When morning came, Christian and I thought we had made

the wrong choice. We were covered with mosquito bites and engaging in a scratch-a-thon, while Phil emerged from the barracks unscathed, except for one red spot on his arm—the result of an encounter with a local spider.

We didn't realize that our mosquito bites would soon be gone, but Phil's spider bite—if that's what it was—would eventually land him in the hospital.

All we knew was that these Lebanese mosquitoes were bloodthirsty little critters.

Incidentally, a few days later, when a Middle East Airlines doctor was allowed to come on the airplane to examine us, he made note of our mosquito bites. Subsequently, we saw newspaper articles alleging that we were being forced to live in a dark, mosquito-infested airplane. That wasn't the case at all. The cabin was dark because we usually kept our window shades down to keep the hot sun out, and the mosquito bites came because our captors had decided to be good to us and allow us to sleep outside, not because they kept us confined to the cabin.

A few nights later, we made another visit to the firehouse, where we were able once again to sit out under the stars and enjoy tea and biscuits. On that particular evening, I had a lengthy conversation with an intelligent young captain in the Amal militia.

He was twenty-six years old and had been a member of the militia almost as long as he could remember. It was clear that he expected to be in the militia for the rest of his life—he foresaw no end to the bloodshed in Lebanon. He spoke perfect English and impressed me with his knowledge on numerous subjects. As we talked, I couldn't help thinking that if he were a young American he might be a surgeon, a lawyer, or an engineer. It was a tragic waste that a young man of such obvious intelligence and ability should devote his life to arms and violence.

I enjoyed my conversation with him immensely, and I'm sure he enjoyed talking to me, too. When the Hisbollah guards wanted to take us back aboard the plane, sometime around midnight, he came back on board with us and sat down next to me, and we continued to talk for another two hours.

I told him that he could have a bright future, and suggested that he ought to try to get into a university so that when the war was over, he could have a suitable career.

He shook his head. "No . . . ," he said slowly, "the fighting won't be over. Not in my lifetime."

He went on to tell me that Lebanon was his country, that he loved her, and he had dedicated his life to serving her the best way he knew how.

"But what do you want?" I asked him. "How can this fighting and killing help Lebanon?"

"All we want is justice," he answered. "We have nothing against the Christians. They're as good as we are. We don't want to throw them out of Lebanon. All we want is a representative government."

He went on to tell me a little bit about the history of Lebanon and explain how the Moslem majority had been excluded from any real share of power in the government.

"People will allow themselves to be pushed only so far," he clenched his fist, "and then they will fight back."

"But still . . . all the violence. . . ."

"What about the violence in America?" he asked. "We read about that. All of the robberies and murders in your cities. Why is it that even your president can't go anywhere unless he is surrounded by Secret Servicemen?"

I leaned back and looked at the ceiling.

"Well. . . ." I was stalling for time. "In answer to that, I can only say that by the rest of the world's standards, we're a pretty young country. We're not that far removed from the frontier, when citizens carried guns to protect themselves.

"Besides that, guns are easy to get in the United States, and it's easy for criminals to get them."

He smiled, nodded, and changed the subject. He started asking me all sorts of technical questions about the aircraft. He understood how the entire fuel system was laid out and how the jet fuel controls worked. His questions showed that he also understood the electrical system and the AC generators.

The more we talked, the more thankful I was that he hadn't been on the airplane during the early stages of the hijacking. We would never have been able to fool him by flipping circuit breakers, turning the engines off, and so forth.

Around two in the morning, he decided that it was time for him to go. But he wanted to leave me with a parting thought.

"Captain," he said, as he rose to his feet, "the United States is the premier, number-one country in the entire world. Everyone knows that!

"You have the most benefits for your people, the freest government, the most possibilities for your people to be successful. You are the model country, the one that all the rest of the world would like to look up to, admire, and imitate."

He went on, "You're such a big, powerful country . . . you shouldn't feel like you have to throw your weight around against a little country like Lebanon. You ought to lead by setting a good example, and then the rest of the world would want to follow."

I started to object, but didn't. I wanted to tell him that the United States doesn't set out to push anyone around. But I remembered the horror stories about the shelling from the *New Jersey* and how many innocent people had been killed.

I didn't agree with everything he was saying, and I knew there were many areas where our disagreement would be deep, indeed. Still, he had given me much to think about. I hoped I had done the same for him.

We were only two insignificant people among millions, but I felt that we had contributed something, no matter how small, to understanding between two warring factions.

We shook hands and said good night.

I watched him leave, hoping that we would be able to talk again . . . and hoping, too, that he would be able to survive the insanity and see peace come to his beloved Lebanon.

Meanwhile, Back in Athens

A few days after the hijacking, I decided that I would have to leave the Hilton and find another place to stay. The Hilton was being besieged by reporters, and I was in no condition to try to talk to them. At the same time, it was wearing me down just trying to keep one step ahead of them.

My support group—Captains Billie and Shattuck, Judy, Carol, Carol's daughter Shelley, Marie—and I all decided that we would move to the Astir Palace. If we were lucky, we would leave the reporters behind at the Hilton, and at least we would be free of that problem. Our attempts to get from the Hilton to the Astir Palace without anyone seeing what we were doing provided the only comic relief of the entire hijacking ordeal. And by that time I was desperately in need of a good laugh.

We finally decided that the women in our group would hail a taxi, ostensibly to take us on a shopping trip. Instead, however, we would be driven to the Astir Palace. Captain Shattuck would be in charge of getting all our bags to the new hotel—and there must have been more than forty of them.

One morning we decided it was time to carry out our plan. We women hailed a taxi and announced very loudly to anyone who may have been listening that we wanted to go to the *Plaka,* a shopping area. Then, once we were aboard, we told the driver we wanted to go to the Astir Palace.

Unfortunately, he didn't seem to speak a word of English. He started talking rapidly and shrugging his shoulders. We could understand the words *Plaka,* and *Astir Palace* but nothing else. He was obviously confused and didn't know which way we wanted him to go. Finally, we got through to him that we did want to go to the Astir Palace, and so we headed off in that direction. But I could see his dark eyes reflected in the rearview mirror, and I knew he was thinking something along the lines of, *These women are crazy!*

Meanwhile, back at the Hilton, Captain Shattuck had called TWA operations and asked if they would send a pickup truck for our belongings. Whomever he spoke to apparently didn't understand what a pickup truck was and sent a moving van instead!

We were gathered on a balcony at the Astir Palace, awaiting the arrival of our bags. Imagine our surprise when a moving van pulled up in front of the hotel, parking in a space usually used by limousines and luxury cars. We were even more surprised when Captain Shattuck jumped out.

"Oh, yeah," Marie looked at me. "This is just great! Nobody will suspect a thing!"

"Very inconspicuous!" Carol chimed in.

All I could do was laugh.

We watched as the bellboy began unloading the bags. There were so many that he couldn't get all of them onto one cart.

But finally he had them all ready to go.

"Okay," he said, "which rooms do these go to?"

"Oh, they're my bags."

The bellboy swept his hand across the huge collection of luggage—suitcases of every shape, size, and color. "All of these . . . are yours?" He cocked his head to one side and looked at Captain Shattuck.

"That's right," the captain answered. "They all go to room 115."

"Okay!"

The bellboy would do whatever he was told. But I was sure I saw him shaking his head as he began pushing one of the carts toward the lobby.

Later on, once all the bags had been deposited safely and the moving van had driven away, we all went downstairs to claim our bags.

I had another laugh when I saw the room. It was a tiny, one-bed room, and it was so full of bags that it looked like a luggage factory. Bags were piled everywhere—on the bed, on the floor, on the dresser—and I wondered what had been going on in that bellboy's head as he was unloading all of them into this tiny room. Talk about taking everything with you but the kitchen sink!

After I was settled in my room, I remembered that I had put a thousand dollars, our vacation money, into a safe-deposit box back at the Hilton. I asked my friend Marie and TWA Captain Jim McIntyre if they would drive me back over there so I could get the money. I thought they could just pull into the loading zone in front of the hotel, I would dash in, get my money, and dash right back out.

But as soon as I ran into the lobby, a reporter saw me, and she was on me faster than you could snap your fingers.

"Mrs. Testrake!" She waved a photograph from the newspaper in front of my face. "Mrs. Testrake! I would like a word with you!" She was thin and tall, perhaps five-ten or more, wearing glasses, and I don't know why, but something about her frightened me.

I tried to walk past her. "I'm sorry, but you must be mistaken."

She picked up her pace, right along side me. "Oh, no, Mrs. Testrake, I am not mistaken, and I insist on having a word with you!"

She tried to grab my arm, and that scared me even more, so I started running. I didn't know where I was going, but I knew I wanted to get away from her. Off to my right was a door marked *Executive Offices.* I ran through it, hoping she wouldn't follow me.

I shut the door behind me and looked out to see if she was coming.

"May I help you?" The voice from behind me made me jump.

I turned around to see the assistant manager of the hotel, sitting at his desk.

"I'm sorry," I panted, "but there's a reporter out there, and she scared me!"

"Oh?" He got up from his desk and walked over to the door.

"See?" I pointed. "That's her!"

"Oh, yes, I recognize her!"

I started to tell him who I was and explain the reason she was trying to corner me, but I didn't have to. He seemed to know me and said he would do whatever he could to help. He spoke flawless English, which was a tremendous comfort in itself.

He shook his head. "I threw her out of here this morning . . . but there's not really anything I can do to keep people out of a public lobby."

When I told him I had merely come in to get my money out

of a safe-deposit box, he had a plan. First of all, he sent someone out to tell Marie and Jim to pull their car around to the back of the hotel. Then he sent someone else to get the money for me. Once that was done, he took me through the deep recesses of the hotel and out the back door.

Even after we got back to the Astir Palace, I was still shaking. I didn't understand, and still don't, why I reacted the way I did. I suppose it was primarily because of the uncertainty of the situation. Who was she? What did she want? For all I knew, she could have been a terrorist. I didn't understand why the news people couldn't just leave me alone. Didn't they understand that I simply couldn't talk to them now?

We heard, three or four days later, that the Hilton lobby was still swarming with reporters, so that made me feel good. Our inconspicuous move across town, although anything but inconspicuous, had been a success.

On the eighth day of the hijacking, I finally decided it was no use sitting in Athens, waiting for something to happen. It was time for me to go home—or at least back to the States. I hated going home without John, but I didn't know what else to do.

TWA arranged it so I could travel as Mrs. Clark Billie.

From Athens, we flew to JFK International Airport in New York. A TWA van, complete with tinted glass to protect my identity, was waiting for me as I left the airplane there. I was taken directly to hangar 12, where the TWA offices are and where John's brother Roger and sister-in-law Margie were waiting. TWA had gone so far as to give Roger a false identity. He was now "Reverend Jones." I didn't know if that was necessary, and neither did the TWA management, but they were doing everything they could do to protect my privacy, and I appreciated it.

I decided to go home with Roger and Margie, to Imlaystown, New Jersey. Imlaystown isn't far from JFK and if, as I hoped, John and the rest of the hostages were released within the next few days, it would be fairly easy to hop aboard a flight back to Athens—or wherever I was supposed to meet him.

Roger and Margie were wonderful to me. They were supportive, and yet they understood when I needed to be alone with my grief. And, beyond all that, they protected me from the reporters who were swarming around their house. They had reporters camping out in their yard and had even had one sleeping on their couch for several days. They had been open and accessible to everyone since the first days of the hijacking, so they had developed an excellent relationship with the media.

That relationship helped them keep my presence there a secret.

Roger told them, in effect, "Listen, guys, we've tried to cooperate with you . . . we've told you everything we can tell you . . . and now we really need some time to ourselves. We hope you understand."

The reporters didn't go away, but they did respect Roger's wishes, and I was grateful.

I spent several days in New Jersey, watching and listening to the all-news stations constantly, hoping to hear the words that would chase the gloomy skies away, but they didn't come.

On the fourth day, I called home to Missouri, to talk to our friends Ken and Pat Larimore, who were house-sitting for us. I was surprised when our son John answered the phone. I hadn't seen Johnny in close to three years. He was not really rebellious, but he had been struggling to "find himself" and decide what he wanted to do with his life. We hadn't heard a great deal from him during that time.

But now, the tragedy of the hijacking had brought him home. He was there to take care of the place, keep the grass mowed, and see that the vineyard was tended.

It was great to hear his voice, and we had a good talk. But

then, with a weary sigh, he said, "Phyllis, I don't know what to do. I can't stay away from my job forever. . . ."

"I know."

I told him I was seeking the Lord's guidance and that I hadn't known exactly what to do either. But now I was feeling sure that it was time for me to come home to Richmond. I hadn't wanted to do that, because I hadn't wanted to face the house. It would be strange to walk in there alone—to sleep in our bed all by myself. I had done it many times before, when John was away on trips, but this was different.

It would be hard, too, to face our friends. I knew that all it would take to make me break down would be to have one close friend tell me she loved me or another ask how I was doing. Still, I had stayed away long enough.

I called Newark International Airport and made reservations for a flight to Kansas City the following day.

It turned out that the manager of the airport was also headed to Kansas City, so he escorted me home.

When I got to Kansas City, I called Pat Larimore, who told me that it was just as I suspected: Our house had been surrounded by reporters since the hijacking began.

"But maybe we can sneak you past them," she said.

I didn't really think so, but there was one thing working in my favor. Pat and Ken both worked in Kansas City, so they could stop by the airport and pick me up after they got off work at five o'clock. That way, at least, nobody would be seen leaving the house at an unusual hour. The Larimores went to work in the morning, and now they were coming home. Johnny wouldn't even have to leave the house . . . so maybe I could sneak in without anyone seeing me.

My heart became increasingly heavy as we drove the fifty miles back to Richmond. It seemed that every landmark we passed, every twist and turn of the road, reminded me of John and the fact that he wasn't with me.

When our house finally came into view, my mind was a

jumble of contradictory emotions. It was good to be home. For weeks—what seemed like years, really—I had been living out of suitcases, and that had taken its toll. But at the same time, the loneliness and despair I felt were overwhelming.

Darkness was just beginning to fall as we turned into our driveway. There were several reporters, perhaps a dozen or more, camped along the road just at the edge of the driveway. I saw a couple of them wave as we drove past, but other than that, nobody paid a whole lot of attention. I felt sorry for them. I knew that they, too, would rather be home. It couldn't be much fun standing around out here in the country all hours of the day and night, just waiting for something to happen. I hoped that very soon they would be able to go back home— and that we would all be able to return to the way life was before this thing had happened.

The next few days dragged by. The best way I can describe them is to say it was like one of those old movies, where time is so heavy you can almost feel it, and the only sound you hear is the heavy ticktock of the clock on the wall.

I cried and I read my Bible, I watched the news, and then it was time to cry some more.

I had dozens of phone calls and quite a few visitors, mostly members of our church, and especially Brian. If it hadn't been for their encouraging words and prayers, I don't know how I would have made it through that time.

And my support group was wonderful! Each time they heard anything that sounded like good news, one of them would call me.

"I heard they put forty thousand pounds of fuel on board! Maybe that means they're getting ready to take off!"

"Sounds like the hijackers are taking a softer line! Maybe they're going to let them go."

When I heard something like that, I would get my spirits up. But each time I was disappointed.

I was especially depressed when I heard government

spokesmen saying that the United States was not willing to negotiate with common criminals.

Ordinarily, I might be in agreement with this approach— even applaud it. But things are different when someone you love is in a life-threatening situation.

All I could think of was the 444 days American prisoners were held hostage in Iran.

When would it ever end?

9

The Lord Is My Shepherd

Dearest Phyllis,

I am just sending letters out in hopes they will eventually get to you—this is the second one addressed to home; the first one I addressed to the Athens Hilton. I just give them to the guards (unsealed, at their request) and after that, I don't know what happens.

Sunday is just getting started in Missouri, but it's pretty well finished here, and absolutely nothing is going on. Our menu continues its wide and interesting variety—supper last night was fried eggs, yogurt in olive oil, and pita bread, breakfast today was cheese and jelly sandwiches (two kinds, not combo), and lunch was special—big thick hamburgers with lots of onion, salad, and fresh fruit.

Phil got bitten by a spider the other night at the militia barracks, and his arm is swollen some, but aside from that we are all

165

completely healthy and in good spirits. As soon as we told them about Phil's arm they sent over a white-robed doctor from Middle East Airlines to treat it. House calls yet!

We are still on the airplane, getting used to it by now, and would just as soon the APU keeps running and we stay here—at least it's a known condition. We have had no contact with the passengers since they left a week ago, so don't know who is best off. We have plenty of seating and the air conditioning works fine. It's kind of expensive—we took on forty thousand pounds of fuel yesterday to run it another week, and I have no idea who is paying for it, except it's not us. I was refolding those few hundred-drachma notes I had in my pocket yesterday, and a guard saw them and relieved me of them, so I now have two dimes and one Lebanese livre. I am learning to be like Paul—content with whatever state I'm in. I'm developing a cozy little rat's nest at seats 15 A, B, and C. Phil is across the way, and Christian a couple rows back. Today I picked the least grungy lav, cleaned it up, and did all my dirty laundry in the sink. Reminded me of washing in a bucket forty years ago in the navy. Then a birdbath for me, followed with a shave, and I was ready for a date. Only nobody asked me.

I woke up this morning feeling especially grateful to God, and thought since it's His day we ought to have some kind of church. So I mentioned it to Christian and he agreed. Since he is a legal Lutheran preacher, he took over the sermon part and I worked on the music (me, of all people!). I got the words down for Psalm 8, Isaiah 6, Isaiah 40:31, and Lamentations 3:22. But got stopped there, as I hadn't marked all the praise songs in my Bible like you did. So if we're here any length of time you will need to send us some more. As it turned out, attendance was slim. Phil didn't join us, and the guards had already prayed to Allah, so it was just the two of us.

Just want you to know that we are both fully committed to seeking after the Lord's face, watching and waiting for His instructions, and willing to do whatever is indicated. From present indications on the news front, it would appear that all men's and governments' plans have just about reached dead end and stalemate, so now maybe He can get this thing resolved in a proper manner.

In the meantime, you can consider that I have been drafted (suddenly!) for some unknown mission and will be gone for the duration, so mail for the boys at the front is of utmost importance! In my first letter, I suggested writing c/o TWA F847, Beirut Airport. But maybe the Red Cross or State Department would be better. You could check on it.

I love you very much,

J

P.S.—I found a Scripture this morning that precisely covers our situation up to now—Deuteronomy 31:6. Tell Brian.

I didn't realize, when I wrote that letter, that Phyllis had discovered Deuteronomy 31:6 for herself, and that she had already told Brian about it. We were thousands of miles apart, and yet we were both given that comforting, encouraging Scripture—one of God's gracious gifts to carry us through this difficult time.

I was spending an increasing amount of time reading my Bible and was also finding strength and peace in choruses such as this one taken from Lamentations 3:22, 23:

> *The steadfast love of the Lord never ceases.*
> *His mercies never come to an end.*
> *They are new every morning,*
> *New every morning.*
> *Great is thy faithfulness, O Lord,*
> *Great is thy faithfulness.*

And this from Isaiah 40:31:

> *They who wait upon the Lord*
> *Shall renew their strength.*
> *They shall mount up*
> *On wings as eagles.*
> *They shall run and not be weary,*
> *They shall walk and not faint,*
> *Teach me Lord, Teach me Lord to wait.*

Every once in a while one of the guards would see me reading the Bible and ask me what I was doing.

"What is that?" he would ask, pointing at the Bible.

"It's my Bible."

"What is Bible?"

"Well . . . it's kind of like your Koran."

"Oh, okay!" And he would walk off. That simple answer seemed to satisfy them, and they didn't display any deep curiosity about it.

Christian tried on several occasions to talk to some of them about the Lord, but they were not a very good audience. They could see that our faith meant a great deal to us, and I hope our actions said some positive things about the God we serve. But at the same time, it was obvious that they were completely sold on Muhammad, and there was very little chance that they would listen to anything we had to say about salvation through Jesus Christ.

Every day, five times a day, the guards would spread their prayer rug on the floor of the cabin and bow toward the tail end of the plane, which pointed in the direction of Mecca.

Interestingly enough, in all the time we were aboard the airplane, they never once tried to talk to us about their religion. They said their prayers, they observed all the rules, but they didn't do anything to try to convert us. I don't believe Moslems work very hard at trying to convert Christians and Jews. Actually, they are quite tolerant of both Christianity and Judaism. They realize that all three have a common origin.

I think sometimes that many people in the West misunderstand what militant Moslems want. Even the most extreme Shi'ites do not want to conquer the world in the name of Muhammad and Allah. They have no desire to "convert" Western Europe or North America at gunpoint, but would isolate their societies from "corrupting" Western influences.

Whenever the guards said their prayers, I was reminded that hundreds and perhaps thousands of Christians also were praying in our behalf. I knew the church group back in Missouri was praying for our safety and release, and I knew that the people in Christian's church were praying for us, too.

Beyond that, I knew that other Christians around the world were praying for us, and I was made stronger by the realization that all those prayers in our behalf were going before God.

It was strange, too, but I did have a sense of peace, as if I were exactly where I was supposed to be. I couldn't understand it, really, but I kept remembering another verse of Scripture, Romans 8:28: "And we know that all things work together for good to them that love God, to them who are the called according to his purpose."

I don't mean to imply that God caused the hijacking to happen. It was a terrible thing from start to finish, and I am convinced that God is not in the business of causing terrible things to happen. But He is very good at taking those terrible incidents and bringing something good out of them. I was always convinced that whatever happened to us, God would bring something good out of it.

After it was all over, I was able to see a number of tremendous things happen as a direct result of the hijacking, but I will talk more about that later.

Sometimes Christian support and encouragement came from some unexpected sources. For instance one day three Middle East Airlines pilots were allowed to come on board the plane to visit with us. It was good to talk shop with them, and it helped us get our minds off the situation at hand.

But when it came time for them to leave, one of them leaned over and whispered, "We are praying for you." The other two nodded, and we could tell that they weren't just saying it. They really were praying for us. We thought that they must be Maronite Christians, and we deeply appreciated their prayers in our behalf. We could tell that they felt especially bad that this was happening to us in Lebanon, their country. It was just another indication that all the people of Lebanon did not approve of what was happening to us. Why, even in Beirut there were Christians praying for our release! It felt good to know that.

But still, we were riding an emotional roller coaster: one day up, the next day down. God was always there to sustain us, but we were tired, antsy, and wanting very much to go home.

We were also trying very hard to keep our belongings together.

When the hijacking had first begun, the hijackers treated the crew members better than the passengers, with regard to stealing from us. They had gone through the cabin, forcibly removing wedding rings, watches, and jewelry from the passengers, but they didn't do that to us. We had to be careful, though, because if we took a watch off and set it down somewhere, chances were it would disappear within a matter of minutes. Also, the hijackers would ask us if they could have our watches, rings, and so on, but when we told them no they didn't force the issue.

One of the guards in particular badgered me often about my Cross pen-and-pencil set.

"Captain Abu Ali, I need souvenir!"

I'd shake my head. "No way! I need my pen to write letters to my wife. Now, what am I going to write with if I give my pen to you?"

He would sigh and slink off, having lost another round. But pretty soon he would be back, telling me again how much he needed my pen for a souvenir.

Part of the problem was that the original guards had picked up all the best loot. New men were coming on board every day, and they were stuck with the leftovers. They all wanted "souvenirs," and, if they happened to be expensive "souvenirs," so much the better.

For the first few days of the hijacking my shoulder bag had remained safely stashed in a corner, and I eventually stopped worrying about it, thinking it was safe. My primary concern was for a brand-new 35-millimeter camera I had bought especially for our anniversary trip.

Then one morning I woke up to find that the bag was gone. I knew enough about the hijackers' methods to assume I could find most of my belongings scattered around the cabin floor with the rest of the high-class "debris." I was right. Over in the corner was my shoulder bag, facedown on the floor, but empty. I found two pairs of socks under 8A. There was some underwear and a uniform shirt under 9B. But no camera.

I hated to lose that camera, and I was steaming.

"You're nothing but a bunch of common thieves!" I railed at them. "You go on and on about your religion, and then you come in here and steal everybody blind!"

I was really hot, and even though they didn't like what I was saying, they made no attempt to shut me up. But then the thought hit me, *You didn't say anything while they were taking things from the passengers. But now that they've started on you, you're getting all upset!*

That made me realize that I was being a bit self-centered. After all, the hostages were all in the same fix. Who was I to think I should have it easier than anybody else? I still didn't like what was going on, but I decided not to be so concerned about my belongings.

Every two or three days after that, my shoulder bag would disappear again. And every time, I would find it facedown on the floor, with my belongings scattered nearby. I may have lost a camera, but through sheer persistence I at least managed to keep most of my personal items together.

Phil and Christian weren't so lucky. Christian was looted until he had lost every pair of socks he had.

I happened to have an extra pair, an old pair of argyles, with a hole or two in them, that I had pulled out of the back of one of my drawers as I was packing for the trip. I had thrown them into the suitcase as an afterthought. I gave them to Christian and he wore them for several days. He still had them on when we were finally released and returned to the United States.

A couple of months later, when I saw him at a dinner honoring the ex-hostages, he ceremoniously returned the socks, which he had washed and neatly folded.

The camera wasn't all I lost. I had about three hundred dollars in my wallet, and that didn't last very long, but at least, I thought, they left my credit cards, my pilot's license, and my passport.

Then, the next day, I found my wallet on the floor, minus the credit cards, pilot's license, and passport. I managed to find my pilot's license on the floor, but the rest of it was gone forever.

But there was still something stuck down inside one of the pockets of the wallet. What could it be?

As I sat in "my section" of the cabin, I poked down into the wallet and pulled out a small Greek drachma note. It had been overlooked, somehow, and was the last little bit of money I had. I sat absentmindedly smoothing it out.

"Give me that!"

One of the guards was standing right above me, his arm stretched out in the direction of the money.

I crunched it back up into a ball and flipped it at him.

"Here you go, buddy."

He stuffed it into his pocket and strode off.

I looked over at Christian, and then at Phil, both of whom rolled their eyes skyward. By this time the constant looting had become almost comical.

I shrugged my shoulders. "Naked I came into the world, and naked I leave." None of the guards seemed to understand what we were laughing about.

By this time I had lost everything of value I had brought on the trip. All I had left was my watch, my wedding ring, and my pen-and-pencil set.

And I realized that I had learned a very important lesson. When my camera disappeared, I had become extremely angry. But the more things I lost, the more I realized I didn't need them anyway.

When it came right down to it, all of these trappings of civilization that we think are so important don't mean anything. When I felt that I didn't have anything else to protect in the way of possessions, it was as if I heard God saying, "Now I have you where I want you!"

As with many other things that happened during the hijacking, our captors meant something for evil, but God meant it for my good. It was a valuable lesson, bringing me to understand in my heart that as long as I had God I had everything I needed.

Even if the hijackers had taken my Bible, they couldn't have hurt me, because I have so much of it committed to memory. On the day I lost that last little bit of money, I realized that if you are depending upon possessions or money, you're bound to fail. But if your trust is in God, and in Him alone, you can't fail, no matter what happens to you here on earth.

That's not to say that I didn't lose some things that were very important to me. Chief among these was a baggage tag that had been given to me when I first went to work for TWA back in 1953. At that time, TWA's name had just been changed to Trans World Airlines from Transcontinental and Western Air, and the baggage tag reflected that heritage.

Many years before, I had put it back in a drawer somewhere and forgotten all about it. But Phyllis found it not long after we were married. She had it nickel-plated, bought new leather straps for it, and then gave it to me as a Christmas present.

When it disappeared, I was heartsick, because something like that could never be replaced, and of everything I lost, it's what I miss the most.

I was also outraged the day my nav kit turned up missing.

A quick search of the cabin produced it. It was lying facedown on the floor, in the usual position, empty. As I picked it up, my anger was aggravated by what they'd done to it. All they had to do to see what was inside, was to release a couple of thumb latches. Instead, the latches had been pried off with a bayonet. The nav kit was broken and totally useless. I couldn't understand it, because the only thing in it were my charts and the technical manual for the airplane, which was missing. Surely none of the hijackers had any use for that. I looked everywhere, but the technical manual was nowhere to be found.

I picked up the nav kit and carried it to the young man who was in charge at the time (who also was the one who kept asking me if he could have my pen-and-pencil set).

"Look at this!" I thundered. "There's nothing in here any of you could possibly want. You just like to destroy things!"

He held his hands up in front of him. "Now, Captain. . . ."

"You're always talking about your religion!" I interrupted. "You try to get us to be sympathetic to your cause, and then you act like a bunch of common thieves!"

He still had his hands up and was backing away from me. But I wasn't finished.

"Why would you want to steal my technical manual for this plane? You can't even read it!"

"Captain! Captain!" he pleaded, "I get you another one! Back in States!"

That response was totally unexpected, and in spite of my attempts to fight it, my anger dissolved in a flood of laughter.

That's the way it went throughout the hijacking. You were either on the verge of laughter or tears, and sometimes both at the same time.

Thursday, the fourteenth day of the hijacking, was not a day for laughter. The latest news about negotiations for our release looked particularly bleak. President Reagan had made some remarks about the hijackers being criminals and thugs, and our guards were steaming. They were so unpredictable you never knew what they would do next, and anything might happen, including the possibility that they might march us out, line us up against a wall, and shoot us. I didn't think they would. But they were angry.

What bothered me most about the sudden turn for the worse was that I had been wanting to talk to Phil about the Lord, but hadn't been able to find an opening. What if something happened to us all, and I had never even tried to talk to him about God? I couldn't let that happen.

Phil is a tremendous human being. In fact, if I had to go through a hijacking, I can't think of two better men to go through it with than Phil and Christian. But I knew that Phil was not a believer. I didn't know how he was able to handle all of this without the Lord's presence in his life. Whether he knew it or not, Phil needed a relationship with God.

Since the earliest days of the hijacking I had been looking for a way to talk to him about the Lord. I had been reading through the Bible, writing down notes that I thought would be particularly relevant to his situation. By this time, I had an entire page full.

I looked over at Phil. He was just sitting in his area, staring straight ahead. Breathing a quick prayer that I wouldn't come on too strong, I moved down the aisle and asked if I could sit down beside him.

"Sure," he motioned for me to be seated.

"Phil," I said, "how'd you like to take out a life insurance policy?"

As soon as he sensed my meaning, I felt an invisible barrier go up between us.

"Listen, Phil," I assured him, "I'm not going to try to jam anything down your throat. That's not God's way. He doesn't force Himself on anyone and I'm not going to force my beliefs on you either."

He didn't respond, so I went on. "This is a piece of good news, and if you want to hear it I'll share it with you. If you don't, I'll leave you alone."

He just looked at me.

"Listen, if you're not interested in this, I'll just get up right now and go on back to my seat."

I started to stand up but he put his hand on my arm. "Now hold on, John. Don't give up on me on this Bible stuff."

"Well, would you mind if I got my Bible and we looked at a few things?"

"No. That would be fine."

I went and got my Bible and my sheet of notes, and we started in. We began in Genesis, looking up all the verses I had written down. I'd turn to a verse, have Phil read it, and then we'd talk about what it meant.

After an hour or so, we had worked our way through the Old Testament and had looked up the first few verses I had marked in the Gospels. But I was afraid of doing too much at once, and I didn't want to turn Phil off by keeping at this too long.

I looked at my watch and said, "We've been at this for a while. Why don't we take a break?"

"Sure," Phil shrugged.

"I want you to think about what we've been reading."

"I will," he promised.

We both stood up, and as we did, I noticed that he was rubbing his arm.

"What are you doing?"

"I don't know. I'm kind of having a problem with that spider bite."

"Let me see it."

On his arm, where he had been bitten by the spider, was an ugly, reddish-purple welt. It looked infected, and it looked bad.

"Hey, that thing doesn't look good! We'd better get someone to come take a look at it."

I called a couple of the guards, and they agreed with my assessment. They immediately put in a call to the Middle East Airlines doctor, and he said he would be there within the hour. It was more like fifteen minutes.

The doctor was a very good guy. He had been on our side from the beginning and had made no attempts to hide his feelings.

He looked at Phil's arm, felt the lymph glands in his neck, and listened to his heart.

Then he shook his head. "I don't know what it was that bit you, but you need to go to the hospital."

The guards objected, but the doctor was insistent.

"This man has to be hospitalized. That's all there is to it!"

He got on the radio and made arrangements to have Phil

transferred to the American Hospital in Beirut. Within the hour, an ambulance had arrived to pick him up.

As we watched Phil being loaded into the ambulance, the doctor sidled over to Christian and me.

"Listen," he said, "why don't you fellows manage to get yourselves sick tomorrow or the next day. I'm sure there'll be room for you in the hospital!

"Just give me a call."

We figured that was much easier said than done. Phil's spider bite was an obvious problem. If Christian and I suddenly became "ill" it wasn't going to fool anyone and would probably only serve to make them more angry.

When I watched Phil leave, I was full of mixed feelings. I was happy that he was able to leave the plane. I knew he would be more comfortable in the hospital, and his spider bite really did need medical attention. But at the same time, I hated to see my crew being broken up. We had been through a lot together, and I think we made as fine a team as I have ever known.

As night closed in I became more and more depressed. I remember thinking that what President Reagan said may have been true, but that I wished he'd waited a few days to say it.

I thought, *This whole thing is going to turn into a stalemate, with everybody calling everybody else names. And here we'll sit in the middle of it, not going anywhere.*

I knew that if I didn't do something about it, this depression was going to get the best of me. It was time to get out my old reliable Bible.

As usual, I found tremendous encouragement in the writings of King David. Many of his Psalms tell of times when he was in deep trouble, surrounded by enemies, and ready to give up, but then God reached down, intervened, and brought him through. I knew that since God is the same yesterday, today, and forever, He was capable of doing for me exactly what He did for King David.

I also found comfort in the writings of James, who tells us to be joyful when we run into various sorts of trials, because those trials are being used to perfect us.

And then there are Paul's words, from 2 Corinthians 4:8, 9: "We are troubled on every side, yet not distressed; we are perplexed, but not in despair; persecuted, but not forsaken; cast down, but not destroyed."

I was also convinced, along with the Apostle Paul, that, "neither death, nor life, nor angels, nor principalities, nor powers, nor things present, nor things to come, nor height, nor depth, nor any other creature, shall be able to separate us from the love of God, which is in Christ Jesus our Lord" (Romans 8:38, 39).

These Scriptures, along with several others, helped me to get a better perspective on our situation. What also helped a great deal was sitting down with Christian and having a time of sharing and prayer together. How grateful I was that there was someone to talk to, someone who understood and who also believed and accepted the promises of God as they are found in the Bible.

Christian, in fact, had used the time of our captivity to read entirely through the Bible, something he had been meaning to do for quite a while but hadn't been able to.

As we prayed, Christian and I resubmitted ourselves to God's will. We told Him that whatever He wanted to do in this situation was fine with us. We knew that the very best thing we could do was relax and trust Him.

After our prayer time together, I felt much better. Things hadn't changed much. Our guards were still angry and upset over President Reagan's remarks, but it didn't seem to matter all that much anymore.

I went back to my area of the cabin, stretched out—as well as I could—went to sleep, and slept peacefully all night.

Early the next morning, I decided to write Phyllis and tell her what had happened:

Dearest,
    Oh, honey, how I am missing you! . . . Like many captives, I spend a lot of time sleeping, and you are spending more and more time in my thoughts. . . .

I would dearly love to be sitting and talking with you on our quiet hill—no gunfire—in our neat, clean house. I may spend about a month doing that.

We are down to two now. Phil's spider bite got worse, and they took him to the American hospital. . . . He was unsure about leaving us but I told him to "GIT!" I suppose if we were smart we would figure out some way to follow him, but we still hate to leave the airplane to its fate. It was a real mess this morning—leftover food, empty cans, dirty dishes, etc. But today we had something new—two cleaning ladies came on board, started in the cockpit, went out the rear door an hour later, and the ship is cleaner than it's been the past two weeks.

We started on week number three this morning, as I am sure you are well aware. Yesterday's paper was full of Reagan talking about his blockade, etc., and the Israelis saying they weren't going to give up their "bargaining chips."

So I had a downer period yesterday P.M.—feeling sorry for myself I suppose—but thanks be to God, He was there with a good fix for me in His Word, and after an hour I was okay again. Some of the Scriptures that did the job for me were 1 Thessalonians 5:16–18; James 1:2; Philippians 4:11; and Hebrews 12:1, 2. Shared all this with Christian, and we had a good prayer time together. So now we realize that when God wants us out of here we will leave, and in the meantime we will wait for any instructions we may need. We both marvel at God's goodness in putting the two of us together in this trial. We could both cope alone, but it's so much more pleasant to have someone who knows what you are talking about. Phil doesn't know, but he's not rejecting it either—he's seen the powerful difference between our attitude and his. I had a nice long witnessing session with him just before he left—we will see what the Lord does with that seed.

I couldn't think of what else to say at that moment, but I knew I would want to add more later on. I set my pen down, folded the letter, and slipped it into the pocket on the back of the seat in front of me.

A while later, the security chief walked past and I stopped him. "We haven't had a shower in five days. What about it?"

He nodded.

"Tonight."

That was all he said, and then he headed for the cockpit.

Good, a trip to the firehouse would be terrific. But what I didn't know was that that night was not going to be an ordinary evening.

Christian and I had resubmitted ourselves to the will of God, and when we did that, things started happening.

10

Whispers of Freedom

Friday night came, and there was no further word about a trip to the firehouse for showers. Eight o'clock, nine o'clock, and ten o'clock came and went.

This wasn't unusual. The guards never seemed to be in a hurry about these things. Maybe we'd go to the firehouse, and maybe we wouldn't. Some of the guards were still bristling over being called thugs and common criminals, and so maybe this would be their way of getting back at President Reagan—make us go a while longer without a shower!

Meanwhile, I was getting sleepy, and so was Christian. We were trying to have a conversation but we both kept yawning, so finally we decided it was time to get to bed.

As I got ready to go to sleep, I heard the roar of a jet engine taking off. I pulled up my window shade and looked out.

A Middle East Airlines 707 was roaring into the Western sky. I didn't know where she was heading, but I envied the people on board and wished I could be with them.

Watching and listening to the planes come and go was not easy for me. I wanted to get back to work, and my thoughts along that line troubled me even more because I knew we were sitting aboard an airplane that was perfectly capable of taking us anywhere we wanted to go. *If only.* . . . But there was no use thinking about it. I just knew that I wouldn't have felt such an agonizing frustration if I hadn't had to hear the sounds of other planes coming and going while we sat there chained to the ground.

Sometimes I would look out and see passengers boarding another airliner. I fantasized about how easy it would be to join them. *All I would have to do*, I thought, *would be to run down the back stairs. Then I could lose myself in the crowd of passengers, and before they could catch me, I'd be on my way to Cairo, or Paris, or anywhere else—it didn't matter just as long as it was a long way from Beirut.*

Thinking about those things and listening to the whine of another jet coming in, I quickly dozed off.

The next thing I knew, one of the guards was shaking me: "Wake up, come on! Time to go!"

I yawned and looked at my watch. It was just after midnight. I'd been asleep less than two hours. Their timing certainly left a lot to be desired. But a shower was a shower. I yawned, rubbed my eyes, and climbed out of my makeshift bed.

Christian was already up, although he, too, was yawning and stretching as he pulled his uniform back on. We both went about gathering up our clean underwear and our shaving kits. Then we would head down the back stairs and be marched to the firehouse, about five hundred yards away.

But this time, something different was going on. We were ushered down the stairs, but when we got to the bottom, a black automobile was waiting for us.

Someone opened the door.

"Get in."

Christian and I squeezed into the backseat, with a guard on either side of us. We were cramped together, still holding our shaving kits and clean underwear. We had no idea what this was all about or where they were taking us.

Once we were safely inside, the car sped off to a far side of the airport terminal, to a place we had not been before, and then drove out through an exit checkpoint. The guard at the checkpoint looked into the car and then waved us on through without speaking.

For the first time, we were actually off the airport property, driving toward the city of Beirut. We turned corner after corner, to the point where it almost seemed that we were going in circles. They were obviously trying to keep us from figuring out where we were headed. They didn't have to try so hard, though, because I was lost in about thirty seconds. I didn't even know in which direction we were going.

We were getting our first real look at the city of Beirut, and even though it was dark, we could see that it was a horrible mess. Here, the street was blasted away or littered with huge chunks of concrete from bombed-out buildings. There, you had to maneuver around burned-out and rusted cars. Debris was heaped everywhere. Luxury hotels with gaping holes in their walls. This was a painfully battered city.

Huge tanks sat in the middle of several intersections, where they could swing their big guns to fire in any direction. Other than the tanks, there was no traffic on the streets. They were totally deserted, and the entire city seemed to be dark except for an occasional streetlight. The only signs of life were the uniformed young militiamen who were keeping watch over the numerous checkpoints.

We would come upon a little sandbagged guard shack, and the car would slow down. Then a soldier would step out, check to see who we were, and wave us on through.

One of the guards knew what we must be thinking and started talking about the way things used to be.

"Beirut used to be a city that never slept," he said as we maneuvered our way around a burned-out taxi. "There was more going on here at night than in the daytime."

He was silent for a while. "You wouldn't know it now, but this used to be quite a city." He shook his head.

After we had driven around for quite some time—at least half an hour—we came into the heart of the city, in an area of little shops and restaurants, and stopped in a small square. The streetlights were dim, but in the pale yellow light I could see several armed men dressed in fatigues lounging around. I don't know how many there were, perhaps a dozen or so, but our arrival prompted them into action, and several of them came walking toward our car.

"Get out," we were ordered.

I looked at Christian. "Is this where we get out and get shot?" I was joking, but I wasn't laughing.

"Beats me!" he answered.

But instead of standing us up against a wall, the guards escorted us to another car and told us to get in, which we did. And as we did, a television crew climbed in with us. There was a reporter, a cameraman, a lighting technician, and all of their equipment, trying to jam into a car with several other people, two of whom—Christian and myself—were desperately in need of a shower. It was not the most pleasant situation.

What in the world was going on here? Christian and I, with shaving kits and clean underwear in tow, weren't in any condition to be starring in a TV show!

But we were in for another long, circuitous drive back through the city. At one point I recognized one of the access roads leading to the airport. But instead of turning onto it, we drove down a side street and parked in front of a luxurious villa that had a high wall running around it.

We sat there for a minute, while the driver got out and went over to the gate. He shook it and pounded on it, but it was locked and would not budge. He walked back to the car shaking his head, and a lengthy discussion in Arabic followed. Nobody seemed to know what to do next.

Finally, they agreed on a plan of action and we took off again. I was hoping that the next place we stopped somebody—anybody—would be home. We had been driving around for more than an hour in the stuffy, crowded car, and I was ready to get out and stretch my legs. We still didn't know who the TV people were, because nobody had explained anything. Our guards were yakking in Arabic, the members of the TV crew were conversing in French, and Christian and I were just sitting there not saying anything at all.

Finally, after another ride of perhaps thirty minutes, we found ourselves in a suburban area of Beirut, where there were apartment buildings on both sides of the street. This time the plan worked the way it was supposed to. We all got out of the car and made our way into a first-floor apartment.

The apartment was nicely but modestly furnished, with a couch, a couple of chairs, and a few end tables. Christian and I were ordered to sit on the couch, while the television crew went about the business of setting up the lights and other equipment.

Once they had everything ready, with the lights glaring down on us, we were given an explanation by the reporter, who spoke to us in French and was interpreted by one of the guards. The television crew had come from Algeria to film an interview that would be broadcast nationwide there.

I looked over at Christian. His hair was sticking out in a hundred different directions, he needed a shave, and he had bags under his eyes which were bloodshot from his being wakened in the middle of the night. Furthermore, his uniform looked like he'd slept in it. I knew that looking at him was like looking in a mirror. We certainly weren't going to reflect the image of two "spit-and-polish" airline officers!

Oh, well, I thought. *It's a good thing I don't know anybody in Algeria. I don't have to be embarrassed about this.*

The interview itself took quite a while because all of their questions had to be translated into English. Then our answers were translated back to them so they could make sure we had understood and given them the information they were after.

I was surprised by the fairness of the interview. There were quite a few heavy political questions, but they didn't seem to be trying to lead us in any particular direction. They wanted to know how we had been treated, whether we thought the Israelis should release their captives, and so on—the typical questions any news reporters might ask.

Christian and I answered as honestly and as carefully as we could, but it was impossible to be totally open, since the room was full of the people who held our lives in their hands. We weren't about to say anything to get ourselves into trouble. After all, we were still hoping for a hot shower once we were through here.

Finally, after about an hour, the interview came to an end. The TV crew thanked us, and we walked out and piled back into the car for what we hoped would be a trip back to the firehouse. Instead, we drove to another area of the city, where we pulled up in front of another apartment building.

Oh, great! Now we'd probably meet with the TV crew from Jordan or Syria or somewhere. But instead, we were taken upstairs to a second-floor apartment. When we entered, we found a room furnished very much like the makeshift TV studio, with one difference: There were two mattresses lying on the living room floor.

When I saw those mattresses, I realized for the first time that something big was happening. Suddenly, the television crew's arrival seemed to be part of a bigger scheme of things. I didn't want to let myself hope that our release might be near—but what other explanation could there be?

"What do you think?" I looked at Christian.

He just shook his head. He, too, was afraid to hope for the best.

The Hisbollah security chief was with us, and that was another good sign. He had come and gone several times during the fifteen days of our ordeal—sixteen now, since it was Saturday morning—but he was clearly in charge of things now.

He invited us to go into the bathroom to shower and shave, which was terrific, because that's what we had thought we were going to do when we'd left the plane three hours earlier.

He waited outside the bathroom door while we took our turns in the shower. Then, when we were finished, he escorted us back into the living room.

He gestured at the mattresses.

"Now you sleep."

"Wait a minute," I said. "This is a pretty dangerous thing to do!"

"Dangerous!"

"We didn't know we were going to be gone so long. We left all the systems running on the airplane. That thing could blow up and burn at any minute unless there's someone on board who knows what he's doing!"

He waved his hand at me. "In the morning! Now . . . you sleep!"

"Okay," I said. "But if it burns up, it's your baby!"

"Okay."

The mattress did feel good. It was almost like a real bed, and I was tired. It didn't take long before I was back home, walking the hills of my farm in my dreams. But I didn't get to stay too long.

"Okay, wake up!"

My eyes didn't want to open, but the voice was persistent. "Time to get up!"

I sat up, disappointed that it had been only a dream, and looked at my watch. It was seven-thirty. We had been asleep for about three hours. I guessed they thought that was enough.

The security chief was carrying a little serving tray, upon which was a silver coffeepot and several demitasse cups. He set it down on an end table and poured out several cups of thick, black Arabic coffee.

We sat around in the living room for a while, drinking coffee and making conversation—Christian, myself, the security chief, and a couple of the other guards. Naturally, there was only one thing on my mind.

"What do you think?" I asked the security chief.

He gave a mysterious smile. "Maybe today," he said.

"Today?" Christian asked.

"*Maybe* today," he said again, with an emphasis on the "maybe."

The words weren't anything new. The guards were always telling us that something would happen "maybe today," or "perhaps tomorrow." But the context was different this time. Something unusual was definitely happening. Furthermore, the way he smiled told me that he knew more than he was willing to say.

"What about the airplane?" he asked, pouring himself another cup of coffee. "Will it fly?"

That was a tough question, primarily because I had been telling the Hisbollah for the past two weeks that the engines were out of commission, and that it would take at least two weeks to fix them. What if I admitted now that the plane would fly, and then they wanted to fly it down to Israel and crash it into the Knesset? Still, that didn't seem very likely. It was time for a decision, and I took a deep breath.

"Well . . ." I said, "I think it will fly. But we'll have to have a Middle East Airlines mechanic go with us and check it over.

"If it checks out okay . . . then, yes, it will fly. But I can't take my passengers—it's not safe for that."

The plane had long since been looted of every piece of safety and emergency equipment, to say nothing of the total lack of maintenance checks.

"No problem," he said. "We fly passengers out on Middle East!"

He drained his cup and stood up.

"We go to the airport, and you check it out!"

I tried to keep a poker face, but a giant crack had just been opened in the veil of secrecy and intrigue that they loved to maintain.

As soon as we were ready, we were escorted downstairs and into the backseat of the car. We were taken immediately to the airport—this time there was none of the driving-in-circles routine—and directly to the Middle East Airlines operations and maintenance offices.

The Middle East Airlines people had been great throughout the hijacking, doing whatever they could to help, and now they were acting as gracious hosts. The airline's vice president of operations was on hand to greet us, along with the maintenance chief and several other dignitaries.

They offered us coffee, and we sat around for a while and enjoyed airline talk and airline people.

"It can be very hard here," one of them said.

He told us there were times when a battle would be raging around the airport and employees couldn't get to work. There would be two or three people on duty—people who had already put in a full day's work—but they couldn't get out of the airport and the second shift couldn't get in!

"We don't give many frills," he said, "but we operate the flights."

From the shot-up, rocket-blasted condition of the airport, I was amazed that they were able to operate at all. Their attitude made it clear that they felt they were a lifeline to the outside world, and they would do everything within their power to keep that lifeline open.

Finally, after we had enjoyed our coffee and conversation, I asked if one of their people could go out with us to look over the airplane. One of the maintenance supervisors agreed to go with us, so he and Christian and I set off across the field, accompanied, as always, by several of the Hisbollah guards.

We decided that I would go up into the cockpit and operate the various controls while Christian and the maintenance supervisor checked the exterior of the aircraft. They had to make sure there were no bullet holes in the wings or bombs hidden away in the gear wells. We were especially concerned about the latter, because terrorists have been known to use bombs that will explode upon reaching a certain altitude or when the landing gear is raised or lowered. We wanted to give the aircraft a thorough going-over.

By now, I was feeling extremely confident that our stay in Beirut was about to end. I could almost taste that tender Missouri catfish!

I sat down in the captain's seat, slid the window open, and Christian and I started calling back and forth as we checked the various controls. I would call out what I was going to do, and then he and the maintenance supervisor would check to see if that piece of equipment was working properly.

Being back in the cockpit and realizing that we were probably on the verge of being released, it was easy to slip back into my captain's mentality.

While we were checking things out, one of the guards came up behind me. This young man had never been one of my favorites. He had an abrasive personality, and I had done my best to avoid him. In fact, he had said to me once or twice, "You don't like me," and I had answered, "Yeah, I like you all right." The truth was, though, that he was something of a loudmouth and particularly fond of expressing his hatred for the United States.

I didn't hear him come up behind me because I was so engrossed in what I was doing.

"What you do?" he asked.

I was right in the middle of something, so I didn't answer. That made him angry.

He leaned over and shouted in my ear, "What you do?"

I whirled around and jabbed my finger in his face. "Shut up!" I roared back.

His eyes grew wide with surprise and he took a step backward. I saw the anger flashing in his eyes. "I kill you!" he screamed. Then he reached over to the flight engineer's panel, grabbed the nearest switch, and flipped it on and off five or six times, just to show me that he was still in charge here. But as he continued flipping the switch, I turned my back on him and went back to checking things out.

He began muttering to himself in Arabic and stormed out of the cockpit. I was sorry that I had yelled at him, because I certainly didn't want to do anything that might jeopardize our release. At the same time, captains don't put up with any garbage from outsiders. I had just let myself slip back into my captain mode a bit too soon.

As we continued with our equipment check, I soon forgot all about the incident. We went over everything we could think of checking and finished up by starting each of the three engines in turn. I'd get them up to idle and then shove them on up to higher power. Amazingly enough, everything checked out beautifully. She deserved an A-plus.

Finally, we were through.

"Okay," I said to the designated guard-in-charge. "It's all right."

"Okay! Get your bags and we go!"

Christian and I knew now that we were leaving the aircraft for good.

"You know," I told him, "we'd better kill this thing completely."

He agreed, so we went into the cockpit and shut off all the systems. We shut down the auxiliary power unit, switched off the radios, turned off the main battery switch—and generally shut down anything that was dependent upon electrical power.

Fat Ali watched as we were doing this.

"What about radio?" he asked.

"No, you can't use the radio," I told him.

"But we need radio!"

I shook my head. "You'll just have to find some other way to communicate."

"But . . . we must talk to tower!" By now a sense of urgency was creeping into his voice.

"I'm sorry," I told him, "but you'll just have to send a jeep to the tower and talk to them that way."

"But I want to talk on radio!" he persisted—like a three-year-old who's been told he can't have another cookie.

"No! You cannot talk on the radio! Motor's off!"

"I use battery!"

We went on like that for several minutes, but I wasn't about to give in. I wouldn't have any control over what they did to the plane once we were gone. But I was going to do everything possible to prevent damage.

Apparently, he finally gave up and walked off muttering under his breath. Mission accomplished, Christian and I went back into the cabin to get the rest of our things together.

But as we were leaving, I happened to look back into the cockpit. Fat Ali was sitting in the captain's seat and he had already turned the master radio switch on. That runs the radio right off the battery and is for use in emergency situations only. If everything else goes dead, you can still get on that number-one VHF radio and communicate. But it won't work for long without draining the battery.

I motioned to Christian. "Look at this guy! We'll have to do something about him. Disconnect the battery!"

No sooner said than done. Christian jumped down the stairs, ducked underneath the belly of the airplane, and opened the access hatch. In less than a minute he had the battery cables unhooked. Now, with the plane as secure as we could possibly make it, we were ready to go.

But there was still one more piece of business to take care of. One of the higher-ranking guards told me he needed to speak to me in private. We walked over to the side, just out of earshot of the others.

"Did you say shut up to Hussein?"

"Yes, I did," I admitted.

"Why you do that?"

"Because he yelled at me, and I don't like people yelling at me."

He nodded as if my explanation of the event satisfied him. "Okay," he said and walked away.

That was all there was to it, but I figured I had gone a bit too far, so I sought the young man out. When I found him, he was still sulking and muttering under his breath.

"Listen," I told him, "I don't have anything against you. You're an okay guy, but I just don't like being yelled at."

He didn't respond.

"I don't like people yelling at me, and you don't like people yelling at you either. Right?"

"Right!" He said it in a pouting, almost defiant manner.

"Okay then," I extended my hand. "We understand each other. Are we friends?"

He looked at me for a few seconds, but then he took my hand and shook it. "Friends!" Later, he asked to have a picture taken with me.

Now, we were ready to go. We threw our bags in the back of the car, climbed in, and headed away from the airport, back into the city. This time, we were taken to some sort of compound. It was a sturdy, thick-walled building with a high wall running all the way around it. The driver pulled up alongside a gate, and we were told to get out.

When the gate swung open, a cheer went up. There, standing in the courtyard of an elementary school, were all of the other hostages—or at least most of them, including Phil, with his arm wrapped in bandages. It was the nicest surprise of the past two weeks.

"Phil! How ya doing? Great to see you!"

There were handshakes and friendly hugs all around.

It had taken us a few hours to complete our business at the airport, and it was now afternoon. Phil told us that he and the other hostages had been brought to the school yard early that morning. At first, the excitement had been running at a fever pitch. But as the day wore on and nothing happened, people began to wonder what was really going on.

It was a hot summer day, too, and the heat was beating down. The courtyard was partially shaded, mostly by the high wall running around the school—but standing around in that heat all morning had taken its toll. The men were feeling wilted and droopy.

Our arrival had caused some renewed excitement, because it was perceived as another sign that release was coming that day. But the problem was that all of the hostages had not yet arrived.

There were four others who had been held in some mysterious hideaway by the Hisbollah. They were supposed to be on their way in, but nobody knew where they were or when they would be arriving. All of the other hostages, except Christian, Phil, and myself, had been in the hands of the Amal. Everyone was beginning to understand that the delay in bringing the final four to the school yard was part of a power struggle between the Hisbollah and the Amal. The Hisbollah were apparently angry over President Reagan's remarks and had chosen this method of expressing it. They didn't want anyone to take their cooperation in this matter for granted. After all, this had been their baby from the beginning.

We were all comparing notes, talking about where we had been and how we had been treated. The members of the airplane's crew were being accorded special "celebrity" status because we had been kept cooped up on the airplane throughout the ordeal. We had not seen any of the passengers since they had been removed from the plane twelve days earlier, but they had all been brought together for press conferences and so had at least communicated in that way.

The courtyard was also filled with newspaper and television reporters. Cameras were whirring, flashbulbs were going off, and it looked like the high-society event of the year.

The reporters knew more about the situation than we did. They were the ones who told us that a deal had been worked out for our release, and that as soon as the other four captives arrived, we would be heading for Damascus.

The way it was explained to me was that we would be held in Damascus until the Israelis released their Shi'ite prisoners. It didn't really matter to me where we were going, just as long as we were getting away from Beirut!

Shortly after our arrival at the school yard, a guard came up and asked Christian and me to follow him. He led us out the gate, across the street, and into the garden of a villa.

This place seemed like a bit of paradise, dropped right into the middle of a war zone. There were brightly colored flowers, a paved patio, and an assortment of expertly trimmed shrubs. How amazing to see this beauty in the middle of such ugliness! It was like God's presence during the worst moments of the hijacking.

Christian and I were brought to the owners of the villa who, along with several other relatives and guests, were seated at tables in the garden. They welcomed us warmly, told us they were happy to have us as their guests, and motioned for us to be seated.

Among the twenty or so people present were several newspaper reporters and photographers. Apparently, we had been brought there primarily for their benefit, because they were furiously scribbling notes and snapping pictures.

As we talked, servants moved among us, pouring tea and offering light hors d'oeuvres. I was probably attacking the hors d'oeuvres like a famished wolf, but I was hungry. I hadn't had anything to eat since supper the night before, and we had been kept awake almost constantly since then.

"Are you hungry?" the owner of the villa asked, smiling at the way I was gobbling down the food.

"Yes, I am."

He called for his servants and gave them an order in Arabic; they disappeared into the house. Within minutes they returned, carrying trays of beautiful Lebanese delights. There were cold cuts, olives, assorted pastries and breads—and I attacked them while the newspaper photographers snapped photograph after photograph.

I knew I was going to look like a pig on the front pages of several newspapers. But I didn't worry about that—it tasted so good!

After Christian and I had eaten our fill, and the newspapermen had all the photos they wanted, it was time to walk back across to the school yard.

There was no news. The four missing men still had not arrived.

We stood around and made small talk while the afternoon moved on. The shadows grew longer, the sun began to sink into the western sky, and still nothing happened.

The four missing men were now the major, if not the only topic of conversation. We couldn't imagine what had happened to them. Were they far off in the Bekaa Valley? Had they been injured or killed? What if the guards told us we'd have to leave without them? We all got together to discuss the matter, and we all felt the same—we wouldn't do it. Either we would all leave, or none of us would leave.

I eventually wound up chatting with Allyn Conwell, a tall, articulate oil executive from Texas, who had become the unofficial spokesman for the rest of the hostages. Allyn impressed me as being a good guy, with an enjoyable sense of humor. His experiences with his captors had been quite a bit like mine—the continuously changing attitudes, the constant assurances of quick release, and so on. The main difference was that the people who had been holding Allyn and his group were more moderate and perhaps a little better educated overall.

While we were talking, a contingent of militiamen arrived, carrying baskets full of food, and everyone sat around on benches

196

to eat. As we were eating, the last shadows of the afternoon grew together into the darkness of evening. It was becoming more obvious to all of us that we wouldn't be going anywhere after all—at least not that day.

After we finished eating, one of the Amal captains came and asked Allyn and me to come with him. He took us out the gate and down the street to another private residence. This one was even more impressive than the home where I had eaten my lunch. Even in the darkness I could see that it was a beautiful place.

An entire family was sitting on the veranda, enjoying the cool evening air. There was a middle-aged married couple, some aunts and uncles, an older woman I took to be the grandmother of the clan, and a young married couple—the new generation.

I didn't really know why we had been brought there. Perhaps they simply wanted to meet a couple of the central characters of the hijacking. The older couple obviously had close and cordial relationships with the Amal, and it was also obvious, from the size and condition of their house and property, that they were very well-off financially.

We sat on the veranda and visited for an hour or so, while their servants poured tea and offered us pastries. Once again, I was struck by the incongruity of this gracious way of life existing in the middle of a city half destroyed by war.

They seemed genuinely interested in us. They wanted to know about our families, what our homes were like, and what we would be doing when we got back to the United States. Several times, the father of the clan expressed his regret that our stay in Beirut had been brought about in such a tragic way.

"We wish you were here because you wanted to be," he said. "Then we could show you proper Lebanese hospitality."

His wife joined in, remembering the way things used to be.

"This was such a good place to live," she said. "The school— there were always children playing along the street—and sometimes we could hear their laughter from the school yard. . . ."

197

While she was talking, her voice trailed off, and her husband reached over and patted her hand.

He began telling us about his friends who had died in the war—some had no real political awareness but died simply because they happened to be in the wrong place at the wrong time. He talked about the beautiful buildings that had been reduced to ashes and rubble. Everyone had stories of horrors they had witnessed or inconveniences they had experienced because of the war.

As we continued to talk, I realized that we were all victims. They were being held hostage every bit as much as we were. But whereas our ordeal was about to end, theirs seemed likely to go on and on and on.

After a while, the talking subsided into silence. There didn't seem to be anything left to say. Wishing the people well, we bid them good night, and walked back down the street to the school yard.

I hoped that the final four pieces of the jigsaw puzzle of our release had been found—but they hadn't. There was still no word on when they might arrive, and it was approaching ten o'clock. Allyn went to the Amal captain and proposed that the operation be called off for the night. Most of the hostages had been hanging around the school yard for twelve hours or so. They were tired, and they needed to get some rest.

The captain agreed, and told Allyn that he would ask for cars to come and take all of us back to our safe houses for the night.

Allyn called everyone together and gave them the news. I expected to hear some groans when he told them that we would be spending another night in Beirut, but there weren't any. I think everybody was too tired—and too conditioned to delay—to react.

Christian, Phil, Allyn, myself, and James McLoughlin, a Roman Catholic priest from Chicago, were teamed up for the night. We were driven to a small apartment, where five mattresses were laid out on the bedroom floor. It had been a long day and I was exhausted. Part of it, I'm sure, was getting keyed up about our release and then having the entire thing fall through. As I lay down on my mattress, I hoped that the next day would not bring more disappointment. But the next day was Sunday—the Lord's Day—it would surely be appropriate to gain our freedom on that special day.

I slept well, but woke up shortly after dawn. I got my Bible and went out into the parlor to have a quiet time with the Lord. I had been reading for forty-five minutes or so when Christian came in.

"Good morning."

"Morning." he answered. "Think this will be the day?"

"It's the Lord's Day, isn't it?"

He chuckled.

"You know I was just thinking that we ought to have some sort of a worship service," I suggested.

"That's a good idea."

"It would be pretty ecumenical, with a Lutheran pastor and a Catholic priest!" I laughed.

"It sounds great to me!"

We waited a while, but we were still the only ones awake. Finally we decided to go ahead and hold our own little worship service. We thanked God for the fact that He had been with us throughout the hijacking. We prayed for our families, for all of the hostages and their families, and we prayed for this once-beautiful country that was now torn and bloody. We also thanked Him for the fact that we would soon be going home.

The morning coffee arrived about that time, and we all sat around sipping and waiting. Mostly, waiting.

Then, about ten o'clock, there was a commotion in the hall. We were about to have visitors, and it sounded as if there were quite a few of them.

The door swung open, and another television crew burst into the apartment, with cameras, lights, tape recorders, and miles of cables. Some of the Amal guards were helping them carry equipment and others were showing them where to set up.

We were happy to see them, not because we were excited about doing another interview—we weren't. But they were Americans, from Cable News Network, and it was great just to see and talk to some people from back home.

"Would you mind giving us an interview?" one of them asked.

"Well, we're not going anywhere," I answered. "And we don't have anything else to do at the moment . . . so sure—fire away!"

I figured we had to be better prepared for this televised interview than we were for the last one!

So we sat down and talked to them for an hour or so. Because they were Americans, and we felt that kinship, we were more open than we had been before. The interviewers asked us some fairly deep political questions, and we all had a chance to say that while we did not agree with their tactics, we had at least gained some understanding and sympathy for the Shi'ite point of view.

It was interesting to me, later, to see Allyn Conwell taking so much flak for his statements of sympathy for the Shi'ites. The fact was that Allyn didn't say anything the rest of us didn't say. Yet, for some reason, our statements were overlooked by those who jumped on Allyn, charging him with being brainwashed and so forth. Allyn was not saying the hijacking was justified. None of us believed that. But at the same time, until the hijacking, none of us really understood what was going on in the Middle East. We didn't understand the reasons for the dissatisfaction and anger in Lebanon and had only vague ideas of what the fighting was all about. Our weeks of captivity had at least given us a better understanding of the situation.

After the interview aired in the United States, I would occasionally receive a letter from someone taking me to task for being deceived by the terrorists. But I didn't get anywhere near the negative response Allyn did, merely for speaking up and telling the truth as he saw it.

When the CNN crew finished the interview, we sat around the apartment, talking about lighter matters for a while. Suddenly, something occurred to me. I felt that I had given these fellows a pretty good interview, so they ought to be willing to do something for me.

The thing that had bothered me most during the seventeen days of the hijacking was that I had not been able to communicate with Phyllis. I had written her letters, but I had no idea if she had received them. I didn't know where she was or how much she knew about what was going on with me, and that was a frustrating feeling.

But here I was, sitting in the same room with a news organization that had contacts all over the world. If anybody could get a message from me to Phyllis, and back from her to me, they could.

"Say," I said, "I've really been wanting to get a message to my wife, just to tell her I'm okay and find out how she's doing. Could you fellows help me do that?"

"Why, sure, I think we can help," the reporter said. "Why don't you just write your message down . . . give it to me, and we'll see what we can do."

So I wrote down a short message—something to the effect that I loved her, that I was all right, and that I would see her very soon.

I then handed the message to the reporter, Jim Clancy, who picked up the phone and called the Commodore Hotel, where the press corps was staying. He dictated the message to someone there and told him to cable it to CNN's Atlanta headquarters. From there, someone would telephone Phyllis, give her the message, get her reply, cable it back to Beirut, and it would be telephoned to us.

"It's on its way," he said as he hung up the phone. "We'll be hearing something back in less than an hour."

Having done that, we resumed our conversation. But all the while we were talking, I kept waiting for the phone to ring. I was nervous and excited—I couldn't wait to have direct word from Phyllis. That would be almost like seeing her in person, although it certainly wasn't going to compare with seeing her smile or looking into her eyes!

Sure enough, just about an hour later, the phone rang. With the first ring, my heart started beating faster. I hoped the news would be good, that she was getting along okay and looking forward to our reunion. I hoped this terrible ordeal hadn't been too hard on her.

But my heart sank as I listened to the one-sided telephone conversation:

"Hmmmmm . . . uh huh . . . uh huh . . . oh." Then he hung up.

"The lady who answers the phone says that Mrs. Testrake is not there."

What lady who answers the phone? I wondered. Couldn't she at least have told me where Phyllis is and how she's doing? Or maybe she doesn't know.

But what had really happened was this: When Phyllis answered the phone, and the caller identified himself as being with the Cable News Network, she didn't know he was calling with a message from me. Instead, she assumed that it was simply another news agency trying to arrange an interview. She didn't want to be interviewed, so she told him that Mrs. Testrake was not home and asked if she could take a message.

"No," he said. "No message. I really need to speak to her in person."

"Well, I'm sorry," she answered, "but that's impossible." End of conversation.

If he had explained to her why he was calling, things would have ended differently.

Phyllis had adopted the strategy of saying Mrs. Testrake wasn't home after she had inadvertently given an interview to the *Kansas City Star*. What had happened was that a reporter called her and asked if she could answer a few questions. When Phyllis answered that she didn't want to give any interviews, the reporter said all she needed was to clear up a few things, such as the proper spelling of our names, our correct address, and so on. Phyllis didn't see any harm in answering questions like that—but by the time she hung up the phone, she had given a lengthy interview. She felt that she had been tricked and was angry about it, so to prevent it from happening again, she just began saying Mrs. Testrake wasn't home.

I was extremely disappointed, of course, that my message hadn't gotten through, but I didn't have much time to think about it.

Close to noon, one of the guards came in with some very good news: The four missing hostages had been found. They were on their way to the school yard, and as soon as we could all get there, we would be on our way to Damascus.

All right! The CNN newsmen were clapping, pounding us on our backs, and we were all hugging and congratulating each other. We had taken a giant step toward home!

We were driven immediately to the school yard, and within the hour all of the other hostages had arrived, except for the missing four, who still weren't there.

Once again, the hours began to drag slowly by, and there was no sign of the men we were waiting for. What was going on here? Was this some sort of cruel psychological game they were playing?

The guards kept insisting that they were on their way, and that they should be arriving at any moment. I couldn't help but think about all the times we had been told, "It looks good! You go home! Maybe tomorrow!" Still, this was different. Sooner or later, they would show up, and this devastating waiting game would be over.

Finally, about four in the afternoon, we heard a commotion outside the courtyard wall. The gates swung open, and, accompanied by a contingent of Hisbollah militiamen, in walked the final four.

The school yard exploded into a spontaneous celebration. You would have thought those four men were returning heroes—and, in fact, they were. The celebrating, whooping, and cheering went on for several minutes, as all the frustrations of seventeen days were released in one joyous outburst.

When things calmed down, everyone was crowding around the final four, wanting to know how they had been treated, where they had been kept, and so forth. It turned out that they had been treated about the same as the rest of us. The only difference was that they had begun to think they were not going to be released with the rest of us. They didn't know why they had been held back, but whatever the reason was, it had been resolved, and we were all deliriously happy.

Outside the school yard, a Red Cross convoy was waiting to take us to Syria. There were at least a dozen cars, perhaps more, with an International Red Cross flag flying from the rear bumper of each one of them.

There were dozens of militiamen, and they seemed to be almost as glad to see us leave as we were to be leaving. I think most of them were genuinely happy for us, that the hijacking was over and that we would soon be reunited with our loved ones. They were congratulating us, slapping us on our backs, and telling us how glad they were that we were going home.

Others were going around handing flowers to all of the departing hostages. One of them came up and thrust a small bouquet into my hand. I didn't know what to do with it, so as soon as I could, I laid it down somewhere.

But as I was getting into my assigned car I was handed another bouquet. There was nothing to do this time except hold on to it.

It had already been decided who was going to ride in which cars. Allyn and I were asked to ride in the lead car along with Reto Meister, the International Red Cross representative from Switzerland. In front of us was an armored vehicle with what looked like an antiaircraft gun mounted on its back. The same sort of armored vehicle followed the last car of the caravan. Amal soldiers manned the big guns, ready to blast away if the need should arise.

Finally, we were all safely in the cars. Someone gave the

signal, and we were under way! As we pulled slowly away from the schoolhouse, I could hear the cheers of the soldiers as they watched us go. News photographers pressed their cameras to the window, jockeying for best position. Television cameramen ran alongside our car for a short distance. Someone was shouting and asking us to please roll down the window, but I wouldn't do it. I regret now that I wasn't more cooperative with the press, but at the time I was just anxious to get the caravan rolling. Other than that, I wanted to be alone with my thoughts.

I also had developed a bit of a bad attitude toward reporters. I looked upon them as being ambulance chasers who were out to make money from other people's misery. I know now that they were only trying to get some information for the folks back home. That night, when members of the hostages' families watched the news, many of them saw their men rolling down their car windows and saying "Hello" and "I feel great!" But my family never saw me, because I wouldn't roll the window down!

It's true, too, that even though the press were there in substantial numbers, I had no idea that there was so much public interest in us. After all, there had been many other hijackings in the past, and I didn't know how much attention the media had devoted to ours. I thought there were constant articles in the *Beirut Daily Star* and the *International Herald Tribune*, but I was not aware that the hijacking had continued to be headline news all over the world. I felt that, by the time of our release, most of the world had even forgotten we existed.

Off we rattled, moving through the streets of Beirut at a snail's pace. We couldn't make very good time, because of the bombed-out condition of the streets. The city wasn't crowded, but there were people standing along the sidewalks, waving and cheering as we drove by. They were doing what they could to let us know that they, too, were delighted that we were going home. I believe that many of them turned out as a way of saying that they had wanted no part of this thing from the beginning. Yes, a Shi'ite mob had marched on the airport while we were there, and there had been other anti-American demonstrations in the city during our forced stay. But not everyone in Beirut had joined in, and now there seemed to be universal joy that our ordeal had come to an end.

It seemed to take hours to wind our way through the city of Beirut. Every fifteen minutes or so, the procession would come to a complete stop, as some traffic snarl had to be untangled. And every time we stopped, reporters and photographers would swarm around us. The city seemed to be full of them.

Finally, Meister asked us if we had been informed as to what would happen from here on out.

"No," I answered. "All I know is that we're on our way to Damascus."

He nodded. "That's correct. And then, tonight, you'll be put aboard an American Air Force jet and flown to West Germany."

West Germany! Allyn and I both let out a whoop. Then we were yelling and hugging each other. For the first time, we understood that this thing was really over, and that we would not be detained in Damascus, as we originally thought.

But after we had celebrated for a few minutes, a strange sadness washed over me, as I realized that not everyone was going home. I thought about young Robert Stethem and the agony his family must have been going through. In the celebration and excitement, I had momentarily forgotten that Stethem had given his life. That tragic, monstrous event seemed so unreal now, lost in the haze as if it had happened years ago. As we continued rumbling through Beirut, I said a silent prayer that God would bless, comfort, and sustain his family through this time of loss.

We were passing through the wealthiest area of Beirut. We were into the hills of the city—hills that are dotted with once-beautiful homes. The driver explained that we were taking a roundabout way from Beirut to Damascus. The main highway between the two cities was closed that day, because of a battle raging back and forth across it, just outside Beirut.

Instead, we wound through the hills and then came back down

the other side, hitting the main highway where it begins its descent into the Bekaa Valley.

The homes in these hills were beautiful works of art—built of stone, with tile roofs and stained glass windows. They were palatial mansions, and yet now they were just junk. There were gaping holes in walls, windows were smashed out, fences had been overturned.

"How many people are still living here?" I asked the driver.

"Perhaps 10 percent of these houses are lived in."

I wondered about these people—where they had gone, and whether they would ever be back to try to pick up the pieces of their lives.

As we got into the hills, we entered an area controlled by the Druse militia. And since we were in their territory, we were going to be under their supervision. The caravan stopped, and we were formally handed over to them.

This was just another example of the difficulty anyone faces in trying to bring unity to Lebanon. Even groups that seem to be fighting for the same things are very protective of their own territory, and it would be difficult indeed to get all of these organizations to agree on any cease-fire or peace proposal.

With the Druse at the controls of the caravan, we began winding down the backside of the hills. We were undisputed king of the road on this Sunday afternoon. If someone was coming in the opposite direction, they had no choice but to pull over and let us pass. If they didn't seem inclined to pull over, they got the message from several rounds of automatic-weapons fire.

Every now and then, we'd hear a burst of such gunfire, and then we would pass a car or truck pulled off to the side of the road with a very frightened-looking driver at the wheel!

Once we made it to the highway, we began picking up speed. But even that road wasn't much. It was a two-lane blacktop road that wound and twisted through the hilly countryside.

A little farther on, we came into the area of Lebanon that is controlled by Syrian troops. Once again, it was time for a change of command.

From that point it would be a straight shot on into Damascus. The land had leveled off, and the road was smooth and straight. We would be able to pick up some speed, and we would cross the border into Syria within the next hour or so.

The Syrians were every bit as trigger-happy as the Amal and the Druse had been. We were going faster now, and the gunfire was almost constant as we barreled through one little town after another.

The sun was descending into the western sky by the time we started back up into the hills at the eastern edge of the Bekaa Valley. Almost as soon as we began climbing we came to the Syrian border.

Once again, there was another transfer of ownership, as we were handed over to the Syrian government. There was quite a contingent waiting for us at the border, including several officials from the United States embassy in Damascus. They were there to welcome us and to give us further information about plans for our trip home.

It felt good to be in Syria, or rather it felt good to be out of Lebanon. I think we were all still afraid to accept this completely; even though we knew in our minds that we were going home, our hearts were afraid to believe it. But all of the things that were happening—crossing the border, visiting with official representatives of the United States government—were signs that we really were going home, and I couldn't stop smiling.

It was around nine or nine-thirty at night when the lights of Damascus first came into view. It had taken us nearly five hours to make an eighty-mile trip. First we would head directly for the Sheraton Hotel, where we would be taking part in a major press conference. From there, we would go to the airport, get on an American Air Force plane, and fly out of the country.

Several high-ranking officials of the Syrian government were on hand at the Sheraton to welcome us, and we were greeted by an enormous press contingent waiting to ask us questions such as "How does it feel to be going home?"

It might have been a silly question, but it was one that I certainly didn't mind answering. I was just delighted that someone was finally able to ask me a question like that.

We were at the Sheraton for no more than a couple of hours and then, shortly after midnight on Monday morning, July 1, it was time to head for the airport and that beautiful USAF C-141 that would carry us to Wiesbaden, West Germany.

Only it wasn't quite so simple. The Red Cross caravan was still waiting for us in the Sheraton's parking lot, and all we had to do was get back into our respective cars and travel the last few miles to the airport. But the Syrian officials wouldn't hear of it. They had played a major part in getting us released, and they wanted to take us to the airport in their vehicles.

We stood around and waited while officials from the Red Cross and the Syrian government discussed the situation. It seemed rather silly to us—we didn't care who drove us to the airport, just as long as *somebody* did. But I suppose the Syrian officials felt that their involvement in our release was a good bit of public relations, and they wanted to take full advantage of it.

Finally, the International Red Cross told the Syrians that if they wanted to take us to the airport, they would have to go through the formal procedure of taking custody. Fine, if that's what it took. What that involved was an exchange of paperwork and a check of the "inventory" to make sure nothing was missing. Because we were the "inventory," a roll call was taken. When it was duly noted that all were present and accounted for, we boarded Syrian-owned school buses and rumbled off toward the airport.

We were deposited on the airport ramp directly behind that big, beautiful C-141, with its huge cargo doors standing open wide to welcome us. The C-141 may not be the sleekest, most glamorous airplane in the world, but on this early Monday morning, it looked like a gift from God Himself—and that's exactly what it was!

There wasn't a great deal of talking and laughing as we walked across the ramp toward the plane. For one thing, it had been another very long day. For another, most of us were lost in our own thoughts and emotions.

But then we were all on board the plane . . . the engines roared to life . . . we were rolling down the runway . . . and suddenly we were lifting up into the dark sky. At that moment a deafening cheer went up—a simultaneous roar from thirty-nine throats that was probably heard in downtown Damascus. Then there was the handshaking, backslapping, and embracing, not to mention a few tears from some men who probably hadn't cried about anything since they were very small boys.

I don't think it's possible to describe the emotion of that moment, when we felt the ground leave us and knew that we were finally, totally free!

Included in the crew were doctors who checked us over quickly and young air force women who served as flight attendants. I have never had finer airline service than on that noisy, drafty, military cargo plane.

Later in the flight, one of the crew members came back and invited me to come up and visit with the pilots in the cockpit. While I was doing so, I told the commander that it would be great if I could get in touch with TWA. I wanted to talk to someone there about the condition of the airplane we had left behind and find out about any plans they might have to retrieve it.

"Maybe we can do that for you," he said.

They had the same high-frequency radios as the ones we use on the airliners, so I told him what frequency to use to pick up a radio relay back to the States. In a couple of minutes he had a radio link directly back to TWA headquarters at Kennedy Airport in New York, and I was chatting with my chief pilot, Ed Stroschein.

I told him that Christian and I had just finished a preflight inspection of the airplane and that it appeared to be in good condition. I also told him that all three of us were willing to go back into Beirut and pick it up—that we thought it was airworthy.

"The only thing," I told him, "is that the hijackers have taken most of the safety equipment, so it couldn't be used for transporting passengers."

Ed didn't think it was a good idea for any of the original crew to go back into Beirut, and told me that instead another crew was headed for Lebanon at that very moment to pick up the aircraft.

"Good," I said. "Because as squirrelly as those guys are down there, you never know how long it will stay in good shape!"

As a matter of fact, a disturbing thing had happened to the airplane just the day before, while we were waiting for our final trip to the school yard.

There are small square emergency exits over each wing. You just pull the release handle and the entire thing pops out. Once the window is removed, an escape rope, which is used to climb down from the wing, is exposed. On board the plane, the three of us had set up housekeeping right in front of these emergency exits. We had tried our best to keep the hijackers from knowing that those exits existed.

One day one of the guards had asked me what they were, and I said, "Oh, that's an emergency exit, but you can only use it if the plane crashes. It's impossible to open it now."

But on the morning of our release, as we had been sitting around the apartment sipping coffee, someone had brought in a copy of the *Beirut Daily Star*. There, on page 1, was a photograph of one of the militiamen walking around on the wing. Apparently, as soon as we had left the area, he popped that window out and climbed out on the wing to take a stroll.

That showed me that the longer the plane sat there, the more trouble there was likely to be. This fellow walking around on the wing didn't know what he was doing. He didn't know where he could put his weight down and where he couldn't step without punching holes in it.

For those reasons, I was relieved to hear that a crew was already headed toward Beirut to pick up the plane.

But later that morning, before the crew arrived in Beirut, the State Department contacted TWA and said they couldn't guarantee the safety of anyone flying in to pick up the aircraft. TWA didn't want to risk anyone's safety, so it was decided to abandon the operation and let the airplane sit there for a while longer. It was nearly two months before a crew finally went in and the aircraft was flown back to the United States.

I enjoyed the rest of my visit with the air force pilots, and then went on back to my seat. I had time to try to catch a little sleep before we got to Frankfurt, but even as tired as I was, I was too excited to sleep for very long.

It was about five-thirty in the morning when we finally touched down at Rhein-Main Air Force Base.

From there we were taken straight to the military hospital in Wiesbaden, where we went through a series of tests and debriefings. Most of my time that morning was spent with two agents of the FBI, who wanted to know everything I could remember about the hijacking.

They were very thorough in their questioning, and I didn't mind because I wanted to help in every way I could. But at the same time, I had been told that Phyllis was on her way across the Atlantic, and that she was due to arrive sometime around noon.

"Listen, guys," I said, "I don't mind answering your questions. But you have to understand one thing. I'm waiting for my wife—and the minute she walks through that door, you guys are walking out."

They laughed, and I said, "I mean it!"

"We know you do!" one of them said. "You've got it! As soon as she arrives, we're out of here."

We talked for another couple of hours, until there was a knock on the door. Then it opened and a familiar face peeked through. It was Captain Clark Billie, and he was wearing a huge smile.

"I have a friend of yours with me," he said. Then he opened the door, and there stood Phyllis—the best thing I had ever seen

212

in my life. The only thing that had happened in our eighteen days of separation was that she had become more beautiful!

I looked at the agents. "So long, guys!"

Without a word, they picked up their things and strode out of the room, leaving Phyllis and me alone.

I looked at her and just smiled, not knowing what to say. I figured something like "Quite an anniversary, wasn't it?" might be appropriate. Or even, "Hello, baby!" But the words wouldn't come.

Then she was in my arms. I couldn't seem to hold her tight enough or find the words to let her know how much I loved her and had missed her. All I knew was at that moment I felt safe and secure. I knew that I had truly come home.

How Phyllis Got the News

Back home In Missouri, the days were dragging, I didn't
have enough energy to do much of anything, but at the
same time I was unable to sleep for more than two or three
hours a night—and those hours came in bits and pieces. I was
up every morning before dawn, and the first thing I always did
upon waking was turn on the radio I kept by my bed and hope
to hear that the hostages were being released.

But on Saturday morning, June 29, when I heard the news
I had been waiting for, I didn't believe it. The radio announcer
said it looked as though the hostages would be freed on that
day, but I just knew, for some reason, that it wasn't going to
happen. The normal thing would have been for me to be
excited, to start packing my clothes and getting ready to fly to
Europe to meet John. Instead, I did nothing.

It wasn't that I was afraid to get my hopes up—I just didn't think it was going to happen. I suppose, looking back on it, that the Lord was preparing me. He knew I couldn't take another heartache.

The next day, I had planned to attend worship services in the little town of Knoxville. Brian Guy was preaching for the first time in a month, and I wanted to hear him. I wanted to go, too, because I hadn't really been out of the house since I had come home, and I needed to get out. Reporters and photographers were still camping outside the house, and I was beginning to feel like a hostage myself.

But when I woke up at three-thirty and flipped on the radio, I heard the announcer saying, "The hostages are going to be on the road to Damascus at any minute." And I thought, *Sure. Sure.* But for the first time, I was beginning to get excited.

I stayed in bed, sleeping off and on until about 8:00 A.M. and by that time the news was looking very good. I decided that I had better cancel my trip to church and just sit by the phone. I knew that if I was going to be flying to Germany that morning I'd have to leave the house by 11:00 A.M.

But nine o'clock came, and still no word. Nine-thirty . . . ten . . . ten-thirty.

Finally, the phone rang, and I heard the words I had been waiting so long to hear. John and the other thirty-eight hostages had just been handed over to the International Red Cross and were on their way to Damascus!

Soon, I was laughing and crying at the same time, as I busily threw my things into a suitcase.

It turned out that there was a direct flight from St. Louis to Frankfurt that left at six-thirty, so I didn't have to be in such a hurry after all. But I couldn't slow down. Within the hour, our three-car caravan was on its way to Kansas City International Airport—with Johnny and me in the middle car.

At the airport, TWA continued to give me the VIP treatment, even providing a special room where I could stay until it was time for my flight to leave. TWA officials understood my need for privacy, and they were continuing to do everything they could to protect me.

From Kansas City it was on to St. Louis, where we met with six other hostage families. We all had a brief press conference there, and I didn't mind it because I wasn't alone. I just didn't want to face the reporters by myself.

All this time, I was feeling very strange. You would think that my mind and heart would have been racing, and I *was* excited. But at the same time, I was so tired. For the previous seventeen days I had been almost afraid to relax and let myself float for a while. But now that the hijacking had been resolved, I felt like I could hibernate for days!

They say it's an eight-hour flight from St. Louis to Frankfurt, but you couldn't prove it by me. Almost as soon as we were in the air, I dozed off—into a serene, peaceful, nightmare-free sleep. I didn't wake up until we were touching down in Germany.

I don't know what I was expecting to see when I was finally taken to the hospital to see John. Perhaps I expected him to be thirty pounds lighter or have a Rip van Winkle-style beard. But when I finally saw him, I couldn't believe how good he looked.

As I rushed into his arms, I was so full of love for him and full of thankfulness to God for bringing him back to me safely, that I felt as if a large balloon were being pumped up inside my chest. It was just so good to be together again!

And I knew that it didn't really matter where we were. Wherever it was, if we were together, it was home.

Back in the U.S.A.

It was one of those occasions when you think you have a million things to say, but then when the time comes you can't remember what they are. And even if you did, you know now that they're not very important anyway.

Besides that, some things are simply beyond the power of words to communicate. That's exactly the way it was when Phyllis walked into that hospital room in Wiesbaden. All I wanted to do was hold her. And as I did, I knew we were communicating soul to soul, spirit to spirit.

The one thing we did do was pray and briefly thank the Lord for bringing us back together. It was at this time that Phyllis shared with me how the Lord had led her to Deuteronomy 31:6 and how she had hung on to that verse as her guarantee that I would be coming back to her unharmed. She suggested that I look it up and read it, and I quoted it to her!

We were both overwhelmed when I told her that I, too, had marked that verse as a guarantee of the Lord's help in my time of trouble. In fact, I reminded her, I had written her a letter in which I mentioned that verse. I had even asked her to tell Brian about it.

"I never got your letter," she said. "But I did call Brian and tell him about that verse . . . when I was still in Athens. He even called a special prayer meeting and built it around Deuteronomy 31:6."

When she told me that, all I could do was lift my eyes toward heaven and say, "Thank You, Lord!"

After fifteen or twenty minutes, we both figured it was time to go find someone and see what the plans were with regard to getting us back to the United States. I opened the door and looked out in the hall. There, waiting patiently, still smiling broadly over the role he had played in reuniting Phyllis and me, was Clark Billie.

He looked at his watch.

"Geez, I've been out here for a couple of hours now! What in the world was going on in there?"

I just laughed, and before I had a chance to come up with a proper reply, he went on.

"So . . . what do you think? You want to stay in the hospital overnight, or would you rather go to a hotel?"

"Hospital?" I must have looked as if I thought he was crazy. "Why in the world would I want to stay in the hospital?"

"Just thought I'd ask," he shrugged. "But I'm glad you answered the way you did. Otherwise we'd have to give the suite to someone else!"

Then he told us that Peter McHugh, who was TWA's vice-president of international operations, had arranged for us to spend the night in his suite at a hotel in downtown Wiesbaden.

"Oh, that's great!" I hugged Phyllis again.

Offering his suite for our use was another thoughtful gesture by McHugh, who had done everything he could to help the hostages' families during the hijacking. Phyllis told me later that early in the ordeal, McHugh came to Athens to tell her and several friends about the latest developments in the hijacking. As he talked to them tears began streaming down his face—he felt so deeply for the men who were being held hostage. Phyllis was touched by his obvious compassion and told me that he was one man who would shatter anyone's preconceptions of the cold-as-ice corporate executive.

Peter had undergone his own bit of testing early in the hijacking, when he had been sent to Algiers as we sat on the ground there. Before his presence could make any difference one way or the other, we took off for Beirut. Peter told me later that watching us take off was one of the worst moments of his life. That's because he is a genuinely caring individual. Now he was proving it again by offering us his hotel suite.

But for the moment, we still had a number of things to do at the hospital. Several dignitaries were on hand to offer their best wishes and congratulations and also to ask enough questions to fill a textbook.

Another feature of the day was a bank of telephones that were set up so the hostages could call their friends and relatives in the United States free of charge. The phones were kept in use most of the day, and I made calls to my mother and our children. I knew that the members of our church had been in constant prayer, not only for my safety, but in behalf of all the hostages, and I wanted Mom and the kids to pass along my thanks and love for all of them.

Captain Billie had told me to let him know when we were ready to head for the hotel, and about five o'clock, I decided it was time.

"Okay," he said. "We can launch the operation now!"

I didn't know that getting to the hotel would be like being in a

James Bond movie, but there were reporters everywhere outside the hospital, and it wouldn't be easy to get past them.

We went down a hall, past military security, took an employees' elevator to the basement, and then left the hospital through a rear exit. Parked just outside that door was a big black Mercedes—with tinted windows so no one could see in.

We piled all our things in the back and took off. We turned out of the alley and onto a street that runs along the side of the hospital. As we drove past, I saw why we were sneaking out this way. The sidewalk was packed with reporters—hundreds of them, with cameras, tape recorders, and other equipment. But all of them were standing with their backs to us, their eyes and cameras trained on the front entrance of the hospital. Nobody even turned around to look at us as we drove past.

Next stop, our hotel.

More problems. A television crew was standing around outside the rear entrance. They were apparently there on a hunch that someone interesting might try to slip in the back way. How could we get past these guys? I didn't want to talk to them—I just wanted to be alone with my wife.

We discussed the situation for a while and decided there was nothing else to do but try to ignore them, so that's what we did. We walked right past them, and they didn't even notice us. For some reason, they all seemed to be looking the other way. As soon as we got to the door, however, they saw us and ran after us. But they were too late. The door locked as it closed behind us, and we were safe. The management was not allowing reporters inside the hotel.

Sorry, fellows, some other time!

We had one terrific celebration in our room that night. There were ten or twelve friends on hand to share our happiness, and share we did. Waiters brought tray upon tray of food—everything from shrimp cocktails to Wiener schnitzel. We had huge amounts of good food, plus good conversation and good friends to go with it. It was an evening to remember, and we told each other that it was the best anniversary party we had ever had—even if it was a couple of weeks late!

Shortly after noon the following day, most of the former hostages climbed aboard a TWA L-1011, to begin the last leg of our journey home. Nine of the hostages had made separate arrangements, but the rest of us would be flying to Andrews Air Force Base to meet with President Reagan. Actually, when we were asked where we wanted to go, the consensus was New York, because it would be easier to get connecting flights to other parts of the country there. But after asking us where we wanted to go, we were told we would be going to Andrews instead, "for security reasons." I personally believe those "security" reasons had more to do with receiving a welcome home from the president, and certainly none of us minded that.

Another consensus on the part of the other hostages was that I should be the official spokesman from here on out. I didn't mind, but at the same time, I didn't want to usurp the position that had been held by Allyn Conwell. But when he agreed that I, as the captain of the airplane, should be the spokesman, I consented to take the job. One of the men had written a statement to the American people and asked me if I would read it at the welcome-home ceremony. I told him I would be happy to do that.

The trip across the Atlantic was a joyful one. Everybody was happy—spirits were soaring. More than one person made mention of the fact that Independence Day was only two days away. This July Fourth was going to have a special meaning for all of us.

It was about three in the afternoon when we finally began our descent into Andrews Air Force Base. There was a large crowd waiting for us there, including my children Diane, Debbie, and Johnny, and my brother Roger and his family. Christian's wife was also there, along with many of the other wives.

When all of those friends and relatives came aboard the plane—well, the only way I can describe it is to say that all heaven broke loose. It was the most happy, joyous occasion you could imagine.

My joy at seeing my own children was almost matched by the pleasure I got from seeing the other happy reunions all about me. Seeing that outpouring of love and happiness was something I wouldn't have wanted to miss!

The celebration hadn't been going on too long when word came that the president's helicopter had landed. He and Mrs. Reagan would be coming on board to meet with us privately, and then we would get off the plane and walk across the tarmac to the place where he would make his welcome-home speech. And, I was told, I would also be expected to say a few words.

I don't remember exactly what the president said when he came on board. He and Nancy met with the crew in the ambassador section of the aircraft first and then went back into the coach section to meet with the other hostages. All I can remember him saying was that he was delighted to have us back, and that many prayers had been offered on our behalf.

I thanked him and told him that we appreciated everything he had done for us. We knew that the situation had been difficult for him, too. There were no easy solutions, and we were all convinced that he had done everything within his power to bring us home safely.

When the president finished talking with everyone on board the aircraft, it was time to move outside for the official speeches. The presidential color guard was there, along with the air force band. Folding chairs had been set up for the audience, and the president was escorted onto a small stage.

He spoke first.

"My remarks will be brief," he said, "if I wait for a second until I swallow the lump in my throat.

"This isn't the time for speeches; this is a time for reunions and families coming together. There's only one thing to say, and I say it from the bottom of my heart in the name of all the people of our country: Welcome home."

Mr. Reagan went on to tell us that the next Saturday would be

Nancy's birthday and added, "She's already declared that you are the greatest birthday present she's ever gotten."

He said that all of America had been concerned about us. He again mentioned the many prayers that had been offered in our behalf, and then said a few words about the death of Robbie Stethem.

"The day your plane was hijacked, the terrorists focused their brutality on a brave young man who was a member of the armed forces of the United States. They beat Robbie Stethem without mercy and shot him to death.

"Our joy at your return is substantial. But so is our pain at what was done to that son of America. I know you care deeply about Robbie Stethem and what was done to him. We will not forget what was done to him. There will be no forgetting. His murderers must be brought to justice."

Then he mentioned the seven other Americans who were, at that time, still being held hostage in Lebanon.

"Nor will we forget the seven Americans who were taken captive before you and who are captive still. They must be released. The homecoming won't be complete until all have come home.

"It's great to have you back where you belong," he concluded. "And thank you, all of you. God bless you all."

Then it was my turn.

"Mr. President, Mrs. Reagan, dignitaries, ladies and gentlemen of the press, families of the ex-hostages, and the people of America. These words were written by one of our men, one of the hostages. He asked me if I would address them to you and I wholeheartedly agree with these sentiments."

A wave of emotion passed over me as I looked out at the faces in front of me, but I kept going:

"Speaking for the thirty-nine ex-hostages, we would like to express our sincere respect and gratitude to President Reagan and the United States government for the continued efforts which resulted in the safe and peaceful end to our difficult situation.

We hope that your efforts will bring back the seven remaining Americans still held very soon.

"Second, to the people of America, we're proud and honored knowing how you joined together in our time of crisis to let it be known that our country was behind us 100 percent. It was your thoughts and prayers that gave us strength and kept our minds on our main goal—freedom. We are now free and want to take this opportunity to thank and applaud you."

I looked up from the paper.

"And just in closing I'd like to say that many of my fellow hostages share with me the profound conviction that it was our Father God who brought us through this ordeal safely. And in the spirit of giving credit where credit is due, I just wonder if you'd join with me in a brief word of thanks to the Lord."

I bowed my head and began praying, "Our Father . . . we just gather before You in humble adoration and praise and thanks. For we know that it was Your strong hands that held us safely through this ordeal, that gave us the courage and the strength to withstand in the darkest times.

"And so, Father, we just thank You for this and we give You all the praise and the glory, through Jesus, Amen."

I didn't know how the media would react to my prayer, but I didn't care anyway. My heart was overflowing with thankfulness to God, and that was a perfect time to show it. Afterwards, many people thanked me for that prayer, saying it had expressed what was also on their hearts.

As soon as the welcoming ceremony was over, most of the hostages—or now, ex-hostages—boarded another flight bound for John F. Kennedy International Airport in New York. From there, we would all be heading to our various homes. I was longing to get back to my farm in Missouri, but it wasn't time yet. First, TWA had arranged another press conference, this one with just Christian, Phil, and myself. I was getting quite used to these media affairs and even beginning to feel somewhat comfortable handling reporters' questions.

The New York City press conference was on Wednesday morning at ten, and I was surprised at the number of reporters who turned out to hear from Phil, Christian, and me. I was starting to understand just how much impact our hijacking had had, and I was overwhelmed.

I also was beginning to see how the Lord was going to bring something good out of it all. My statements regarding God's care during the hijacking had not gone unnoticed, even by the "secular" media, and I quickly realized that I was going to be given many opportunities to talk about my faith. Naturally, I was delighted to have a forum to tell others about God's Good News, and how He had seen us through our ordeal. At this time, though, I didn't yet have an understanding of how many times I would be asked to stand up and speak of this. I felt there might be another interview or two when I got home, and then it would stop. How little I knew!

But for now, the reporters in New York City asked dozens of questions. They wanted to know every detail of the hijacking, and even asked Phil to show them his spider bite.

It was all rather exhilarating, but I was delighted when it was over. That meant the time had finally come to go home, and I couldn't wait to get back to Richmond. How I had longed to see those rolling, green hills during those long days trapped on the runway in Beirut. How I had yearned to get out in my vineyard and work up some sore muscles while I had been sitting around with nothing to do but read and sleep!

Phil and Christian were just as anxious to get home as I was— Phil to Utah and Christian to Idaho.

"Well, gentlemen," I said, as we shook hands good-bye. "It certainly has been a memorable trip!"

They both nodded in agreement. "Let's hope the next one is kind of dull," Phil said.

Christian laughed. "It's been great working with you two. Maybe I'll get the chance to do it again."

"I hope so!" I told him.

And with that, we all went our separate ways.

It was mid-afternoon when we landed at Kansas City International Airport, and quite a few of our family and friends were there to greet us, including Ken and Pat Larimore, who would drive us back to Richmond in their long, red convertible. Several other members of the community had come down to welcome us home and still others, they informed me, were busy helping to arrange a "proper" welcome in Richmond.

"But can't a man just quietly sneak back into town?" I smiled. Frankly, I was becoming embarrassed by all the attention. But I was going to have to get used to it, because once more, I was facing a room full of reporters.

I tried to be attentive, polite, and answer all their questions, but I was beginning to tire of answering the same questions over and over. And here we had only been free for a little more than two days!

There was one question, though, that was new.

"Captain Testrake," someone asked, "what's the first thing you're going to do when you get home?"

The answer to that was easy. Early the next morning, I was going to drive down to the barbershop and get my hair cut. If being home with my family sounded like paradise, getting my shaggy hair cut was certainly the next best thing! One understands how much simple things like haircuts mean when they are taken away. That sounds like a cliché. It's also true.

When the press conference was finally over, and we had been officially welcomed back to Missouri, it was time for our small caravan of cars to head out on the road to Richmond. I had driven Route 291 many times before, but it had never seemed so much like an old friend.

As he drove along, Ken pointed to the many yellow ribbons that seemed to be everywhere—on mailboxes, trees, fence posts, shrubs—visible signs of the love and support from my Missouri neighbors. The small lump in my throat was getting bigger all the time. Phyllis, too, was touched, and I could see the mist forming in her eyes.

It wasn't just ribbons, either. There were people standing here and there along the road, waving at us as we drove past. These were country roads, far from any cities, and yet the people had come from their farms and from nearby towns, just so they could see us go past—just to wave and smile and let us know how happy they were that the hijacking was over and I was safely home.

As we drew closer to Richmond, there were more and more people, waving, cheering, and holding banners that read *Welcome home, John* and *We love you, John!* It was absolutely beautiful!

I suppose I felt a little bit like someone who had died and gone to his own funeral, where he heard all the nice things people were saying about him. I was touched and happy, and yet embarrassed and humbled by all the attention.

What I had seen so far was only a small foretaste of what was to come. When our caravan made its way into Richmond, it looked as though the entire town had been tied up in a bright, yellow bow. There were ribbons everywhere! And as we motored into the town square, it became obvious that the whole town had turned out to meet us.

Richmond has a few more than five thousand residents, and there were nearly four thousand people crammed into the town square that day. The high school band was playing, balloons floated in the breeze, aircraft circled overhead, and everywhere I looked banners proclaimed their messages of welcome and rejoicing at my safe return.

The mayor made a speech; the publisher of the local paper was there. And, so, too, were the ever-present reporters and television cameras.

It was a spectacular celebration, and one that I appreciated very much. But still, I was happy when it was over. Now I could finally get home to my farm and go back to being plain old John Testrake.

Or so I thought. If there were any people in Richmond who hadn't been at the celebration downtown, I found out where they were: in my front yard! Once again, there were yellow ribbons and banners to welcome me home, a crowd of well-wishers, and—more reporters. I was beginning to wonder exactly how many reporters there are in the world.

As Ken guided the red convertible up the driveway, I thought, once again, that I had never seen the farm looking so good. Seeing the house sitting on that hillside was like having my best dream turned into reality. What a feeling!

Ken parked in the driveway, and I quickly jumped out ahead of everyone else. I wanted to see my vineyard, so I walked straight out to the side yard, where I could look out over the farm. A swarm of reporters followed along behind me, bombarding me with questions such as "How does it feel to be home?" and "Do you have any special words for our readers?"

"I feel great!" I told them. "It's so good to be back home in Missouri, where I can relax and have peace and quiet."

I turned and looked at the mob behind me. It seemed a little ridiculous to be talking about peace and quiet with this group yelling questions at me, and cameras recording every move I made.

"Listen, folks," I said. "I'll see you around, okay? Good-bye!"

I was surprised at their reaction. "Thank you, Captain Testrake," and they turned to leave. I couldn't believe how cooperative they were. They understood that I wanted to be alone, and they were willing to give me what I wanted.

That evening, it was just my family and a few selected guests, sitting around talking about the hijacking, as well as what had been going on here at home during the last two and a half weeks.

Sometime during the evening, I realized that I had made a goof during the press conference in Kansas City.

Oh, no! I thought. *Everyone must have thought I was crazy when I said I was going to get a haircut tomorrow. Tomorrow's the Fourth of July. Barbershops aren't open on the Fourth of July.*

230

I also realized that Richmond usually celebrates Independence Day in a big way.

I hoped this year would be different, but thought I should call Howard Hill, the publisher of the local newspaper, and ask him if anything was planned.

"No, John," he told me. "We pulled out all the stops today, and there's nothing at all going on tomorrow."

"Ah . . . that's wonderful," I sighed. "I was hoping to just take it easy here at home."

We stayed up talking and laughing and having a wonderful time that night, until well past our usual bedtime. And then I enjoyed a wonderful night's sleep that I can only describe as "delicious." I don't know when I have ever enjoyed a night's sleep more. I was at home, in my own bed, with the love of my life, my wife, beside me—and it was absolutely marvelous! I woke up a couple of times during the night, and each time I did, the first thought across my mind was how very good it felt to be in that bed. And then I'd drift back to sleep, smiling in the dark.

Just after 8:00 A.M. the phone rang.

"John, where are you? I'm ready to cut your hair."

It was Mae Hammond, owner of the barbershop where I always get my hair cut.

"Oh, Mae," I said. "I forgot completely about it being the Fourth of July."

"Well, that's okay. . . . ."

"No, Mae, listen. I'm sorry. I'll come see you tomorrow."

"Now, John," she scolded, "I'm here waiting for you, and you get over here to this barbershop right now!"

I knew better than to disobey her orders.

"Yes, ma'am, I'll be right there."

"Besides," she gave me a parting shot, "you're getting awful shaggy!"

And so Independence Day found me doing just what I'd said I'd do—getting my hair cut and reflecting on the cooperative spirit and friendly nature of people in small-town America.

As I settled myself into Mae's barber chair, I was surprised to see a TV crew come rolling in. The Kansas City stations still had film units in the area looking for newsworthy happenings, and they had apparently seen me walk into the barbershop. That marked the first time my getting a haircut had ever been front-page news.

Good grief! I thought. *When is this sort of thing going to end? When can I go back to being a private citizen?*

I got another taste of what it was like to be a "celebrity" a few days later, when Phyllis and I headed back to New York for the fortieth reunion of my high school graduating class. It was a chance to see my mother, and I had been planning the trip since before the hijacking.

The night of the dinner, the TV people were waiting in front of the restaurant. They were rolling tape as Phyllis and I got out of the car, and then they followed us into the restaurant, recording everything we did and said.

The following morning was Sunday and I was to be the guest of honor at the Methodist Church where I had first attended Sunday school as a child. I was looking forward to that, especially because it would give me a chance to tell the people there how good God had been to me throughout the hijacking, giving me a sense of His presence and the certain knowledge of His care.

However, when we arrived at the little church, there, again, were the television cameras.

They were set up outside the church for our arrival, and then they followed us on into the building. Inside, the pastor's wife was visibly upset and arguing with a man who must have been the executive producer. The minister was conducting early services elsewhere, and the producer was trying to rearrange the interior of the church to suit his purposes.

"We'll have these lights over here," he was telling her, as he marched back and forth in the front of the church, "and then the minister can stand here . . . and Captain Testrake over this way."

"But that's not the way—" she protested.

232

"Well, now, honey . . . we can't do it that way!"

"This is a house of worship," she countered. "We're here to worship the Lord, and that's what we're going to do. We're not here to do a TV show."

"But you don't understand," he protested.

"Sir! YOU do not understand!" She insisted, and he finally had to back down and do it her way. Having the TV crew filming during the worship service was enough of an intrusion—she wasn't about to let them disrupt and rearrange things any more than was absolutely necessary.

I was happy to see her stick to her guns and told her so. I could tell from talking to her that she was a sensitive person who didn't like to get angry and have to deal with someone in that way, but I thanked her and told her that I thought she had done exactly what needed to be done.

The service proceeded normally after that, but when it was over, there were more reporters waiting out in front of the church for another press conference. Also there were several officials of the town and county, who presented me with plaques of appreciation. As a final touch, we rode in a parade, down the main street of my original hometown.

A family reunion was planned for that afternoon at my aunt's house, and when I told the reporters about it, they all wanted to come. But I couldn't have them there. The family deserved some privacy, and I told them so. I hadn't even meant to mention it to them. It was just one of those things:

"Captain Testrake, where do you go from here?"

"Well, this afternoon, I'll be attending a reunion at my aunt's house, and. . . ." It's a little bit like toothpaste—once you've let it out, there's nothing you can do to get it back into the tube. One thing I learned very early in my dealings with the media is that you really have to admire those politicians who can dance around all the tough questions. It's not an easy thing to do.

But when I told the reporters that I was sorry but they weren't invited to the reunion, they accepted it. Having the cameras and tape recorders going all the time was annoying, and yet the reporters and photographers did seem to respect my privacy. When I told them that enough was enough, they backed off. Of course, some of that was probably because I was being regarded as something of a hero, so they went out of their way to cooperate with me.

When things were over in New York, we headed back to Richmond. Surely, I thought, things were about to quiet down, but no such luck.

The phone was ringing as we walked through the door of our house, and that was a portent of things to come.

One minister called, wanting me to speak at his church. A Kiwanis program chairman needed me to come speak to his group. A veterans' organization asked me to be the featured speaker at their banquet. And on and on it went.

I didn't know how to handle it, and I hated turning people down. But my calendar began filling up very quickly, and very far in advance. I would find myself at eleven in the morning, still in my bathrobe, unshaven, not even having had a chance to comb my hair—and talking long-distance on the telephone.

This routine went on for a couple of weeks, until Phyllis had totally lost her patience. (And that, I must add, does not happen easily.)

It was one of those mornings when I had been on the phone for hours, and I had just finished the latest conversation. Before the phone could ring again, she ran over, grabbed it, and dialed the business office.

"Get us an unlisted number!" she demanded.

That helped to cut back on the number of telephone calls, but it was surprising how many people still managed to get the unlisted number somehow.

We kept thinking it was going to die down, but it didn't. I was most inclined to accept the invitations that came from churches, because I knew I would get a chance there to share openly about

God's love and protection. But there was just no way I could accept even all of those invitations.

Letters came pouring in, too, mostly from people wanting me to know that they had been praying for me during my captivity or telling me that my calm attitude in the face of danger had been an inspiration to them. I wished that they all could understand that it was only the Lord's presence in the situation that allowed me to remain calm. Among the letters were several from old friends, people I had lost contact with over the years, but who wanted to let me know that they, too, had been praying for me and were delighted when I returned to the United States. I wanted to answer all of the mail, but of course that was impossible. There was barely time to read it all!

The flood of invitations was finally curtailed somewhat when Larry Hilliard took over the task of sorting through them. Larry later became vice-president of corporate communications for TWA, but at that time he was director of public relations in Kansas City. The airline arranged for all inquiries to be directed through Larry, who would screen them and toss out any that he knew I wouldn't be interested in. Every so often he would call me and say, "John, I've got half a dozen things I want to run by you, and if you're interested in any of them let me know and we can set it up." I was delighted to have Larry's help, because it made my life much easier.

Through all of the whirlwind—traveling around the country making speeches and wading through huge stacks of mail—I was beginning to see that God was bringing several good things out of the hijacking. The most important was that the incident gave me a chance to tell others about His goodness. It gave me instant recognition, which meant that people would listen to what I had to say. They would also listen to me because they knew I'd experienced firsthand what I was talking about. You can talk all day about God's care in time of trouble, but if you've never had trouble, people can always walk away thinking that you don't know what you're talking about.

But when you've been face to face with death and God has brought you safely through, they'll listen. And it hasn't been only in the churches where I've had a chance to talk about God's goodness. Almost every time I speak, I am asked again what sustained me during the ordeal, and I always answer without hesitation that it was the reassuring presence of God's Spirit, the "peace that passes all understanding."

On one such occasion, Phyllis and I were invited to New York City, where I was to speak before the Wings Club, an organization made up of pilots and other professionals from the field of aviation. As a part of our time with the Wings Club, we were invited to a cocktail party on the Upper East Side of Manhattan—a very elegant affair.

During the course of the evening, Phyllis was talking with some of the women, and the conversation came around to our faith in the Lord. Phyllis was able to tell them how He sustains us and lifts us up, and she quickly found herself the center of attention. They wanted to hear more and asked her question after question regarding the things God has done in our lives. I don't know if they went out and gave their lives to Jesus, but at least the seeds were planted.

Then the time came for me to speak before the group, in the big ballroom of the Grand Hyatt Hotel. I hadn't planned on talking about my faith that day, because I knew the members of the Wings Club would really be interested only in the technical aspects of the hijacking. After all, these were people who were intimately involved with the aviation industry.

But at the end of my speech, I offered to answer any questions from the floor.

Here it came again. A man stood up and asked, "Captain, could you give us any idea as to what it was that really sustained you and gave you the strength and the courage to come through this thing?"

Well . . . I hadn't really planned on talking about it, but I couldn't let an opportunity like that get away. So I told him. And the 350-plus members of the Wings Club gave me a standing ovation. They were genuinely touched, and I was astonished by their response, especially in such a "sophisticated" and "cynical" place as New York City.

Some other good things that came out of the hijacking are of a more personal nature. For instance I, myself, learned some important lessons about God's protection and care. I knew all those things theoretically before, but now I have experienced them firsthand. The hijacking also enabled me to renew some acquaintances with old friends, and that has been a most enjoyable aspect of the adventure. And, finally, the hijacking served to bring my family together. We are much, much closer now. It's as if we all went through the hijacking together, and we gained a strength and a unity from it that we will not lose.

Before the hijacking, for instance, I hadn't seen my younger son, Johnny, in nearly two years. But the hijacking reminded him that he had a family who cared about him, and it also reminded him that he cared about us.

When Johnny was growing up, it looked very much as if he would be the one to follow in my footsteps. I think nearly every father hopes to see his son going into the "family business," and I was no exception. When Johnny was young, he'd had a keen interest in aviation, and I enjoyed talking about airplanes with him. There was little doubt in my mind that he was cut out to be a pilot. He went to airshows with me and was quick to grasp the terminology and technology of aviation. Furthermore, he was healthy and had excellent vision. In short, he seemed to be a natural.

But then, when he was fourteen, he lost interest altogether. Aviation dropped completely from his list of "interests."

I wasn't sure what caused it, whether it was the death of his mother, or the feeling every young man goes through, when he wants to find his own niche in life, but I knew better than to push him toward aviation. Besides, this was a time when the future did not look tremendously bright for the airlines. Fuel prices were skyrocketing, which was sending airline profits into a downward spiral. Things didn't look as bright for a young man going into flying as they had in my day. This, too, was something Johnny understood.

I was disappointed by his sudden lack of interest in flying, of course, but knew that he had to make up his own mind regarding what he wanted to do with his life.

And it was obvious that he had a tremendous aptitude for music. As a member of his high school band, Johnny had picked up several all-state awards for his musicianship. Music had become his number-one passion, and that was fine with me, because he was very good at it. He also worked hard—he wanted to be better and better, and I was proud of his many achievements.

Upon graduation from high school, he decided to join the air force, but even there, he didn't do any flying. I wondered, when he joined the air force, whether his old interest in aviation was being rekindled, but he served his entire three-year stint without flying once!

When that was up, he remained in Florida, where he joined a rock 'n' roll band looking for fame and fortune. He was playing with the band when the hijacking occurred, and, as I said earlier, we hadn't seen him in two years.

That's why Phyllis was surprised to hear him answer the phone when she called home during the hijacking. As soon as he'd heard about it, Johnny had come back to Richmond. He had been mowing the lawn, looking after the vineyard, and doing everything he could to help keep the house in shape.

When I finally came home, Johnny and I sat out on the back patio and talked things over. He was becoming discouraged with his life in the band. He still loved music, but he was discovering that very few musical groups ever find the way to fame and fortune.

"Boy, Dad," he told me, "I sure wish I'd gone into flying."

"Well, you know, you still can."

"Now?"

"Sure!" I told him. "If you had learned to fly back when you were seventeen or eighteen years old, you might not have been able to get a job, but now you can."

"Really?"

Johnny had no idea that conditions in the airlines had improved. He remembered the hiring freezes and cutbacks of years gone by and thought that was still the way things were.

We sat there for a moment while he absorbed this new bit of information.

"But where can I learn to fly?" he asked.

"Oh, there are any number of good schools," I answered. "One of the best I know of is just forty minutes down the road at Central Missouri State University."

The more we talked about it, the more I could see his interest building. He finally decided that enrolling in aviation school was exactly what he wanted to do. He could go back to Florida to take care of business with his band, and while he was there, he would check out some commercial aviation schools. Then he would also take a look at Central Missouri State's program.

By September, he was enrolled in the school there. During the next year, he picked up more than four hundred hours of flying time, and he's well on his way to becoming a top-notch pilot. I fully expect that someday he will be sitting in the captain's seat.

Johnny's renewed interest in flying makes me proud, because it's good to see something that means so much to me beginning to mean a great deal to him. Furthermore, because he enjoys flying as much as he does, it's obvious to both of us that this is what he should have been doing all along. If the hijacking had not occurred, he may never have discovered that.

No, the hijacking was not a good thing by any stretch of the imagination. It was a horrible, brutal, evil thing. The sort of thing that only a magnificent God could use for good.

And I can tell you from firsthand experience, that is the kind of God we serve!

13

Reflections

As the hijacking of TWA Flight 847 fades into history, I find my life getting back to normal, albeit with a heightened sense of enjoyment. I had begun to forget, I suppose, how much I enjoy flying. Now, when I'm flying off to San Francisco or London, or wherever it may be, I am reminded of the fact that I'm doing exactly what I've always wanted to do. There is a new appreciation of the star-studded night sky from high over the Great Plains, a fresh sense of satisfaction in a perfect landfall off the Irish coast.

The hijack also opened my eyes to the joys of day-to-day life. I've always enjoyed my farm and working in my vineyard, but now there is a new intensity to that. And my wife, my children, the other members of my family, my friends—all of these people are loved and cherished in a special way since the hijacking.

Our church, Christian Fellowship Ministry, attempts to follow Jesus' example in welcoming and loving the lost and homeless, and I find that I cherish these people in a new way, too. I recognize that there are many cracks and blemishes in my own makeup, and that any confidence or skill I possess comes from God and not from my own capabilities. This makes it easy to see past the occasional harsh surface features in others and to look for the good God finds in every one of His children.

I find it natural to extend this same principle to include nations and cultures that are different from our own. Our human impulse is to show mistrust and hostility to those different from ourselves, but a close, impartial look shows people everywhere to be very similar in basic makeup. Looking past man-made barriers, traditions, and differences, we can see that all people have the same mix of good and bad, the same basic impulses. All are subject to pride, fear, suspicion, envy, jealousy, and hate, but all are also equally motivated by the desire to protect and provide for the family, to have a sense of self-worth, and to be free from domination by others.

In short, I enjoy a fresh appreciation of life and of people, and I no longer take either for granted. There has been a heightened awareness that God is about His business of bringing good out of evil. I was filled with the sense of His presence and His protective hand throughout the otherwise frightening events on board the aircraft, and I can see His influence in our lives since then. All these things have brought me closer to God and shown me new insights into His marvelous character.

Since my return to the United States, I have been amazed at how many of my fellow pilots have come up and thanked me for the way I conducted myself during the hijacking. Specifically, many of them were delighted to hear me speak up for the Lord.

I have also been surprised to discover the worldwide interest and concern the hijacking generated.

During our captivity, we had looked upon the event as just

another hijacking: a brief bit of violence flaring up today and forgotten tomorrow. But that has not been the case.

Once we were past the dazzling array of press conferences, parades, and speeches, we returned home to find a flood of mail from all around the world—from Korea to Paris, from the Faeroe Islands in the North Atlantic to Tasmania in the South Pacific.

Almost all of the writers spoke of heartfelt prayers to God on our behalf and of gratitude to Him for hearing and answering. Requests for television and speaking appearances poured in. That was perhaps understandable given the amount of media coverage devoted to the event. But what is startling is that this attention has not disappeared with the passing of time. Passengers still respond when my name is announced by the flight attendants on the aircraft public address system, and they generally want to thank me for representing America well.

Requests continue to come in for speaking engagements. Most are not major events—they are from aviation groups, churches, colleges, civic groups, and so on. All requests are treated equally, for I quickly learned that the most gratifying results often come from the most obscure places.

The statement I made in one of my letters to Phyllis still applies: "I have apparently been drafted for some unknown mission and will be gone for the duration."

The only difference is that now my wife has joined me, and we are ready for any service that may be indicated. We have become acquainted with the phrase, "God does not require brilliant people, only faithful ones." And so we have attempted to be faithful and to follow wherever He has chosen to lead us.

Meanwhile, I thank God for allowing me to spend so much of my life doing something I love—flying.

I have always loved flying and I always will. No group of terrorists could change that. And the next time I visit Athens or the Middle East, I will be reminded of only one thing: God's protection and presence in times of trouble.

Epilogue:
Frequently Asked Questions

Whenever I speak, I like to take a few moments to ask for questions from the audience. I have discovered that certain questions are asked repeatedly. A few of those questions, and my answers, follow.

Are you still flying?

Yes. In fact, I had to get back in the cockpit just to get some peace and quiet—to get away from the ringing telephone, the requests for interviews, and so on. In addition, I am rapidly approaching the FAA mandatory retirement age of sixty, so I don't have a lot of time left in the career I love so much.

How much time off did the airline give you following the hijacking?

I was told to take as much time as I wanted, but after a month I was ready to get back to the peace and quiet of flying.

Where are you flying?

My preference would be to fly international routes, but because of a decrease in the number of Americans making trips overseas I have been flying transcontinental routes.

Aren't you afraid to fly overseas?

No. It's much safer than driving to the airport. The media does such a conscientious job of fully reporting every gory detail of each terrorist incident while completely ignoring the thousands of trips peacefully flown each and every day (no violence there) that the true peril is blown completely out of perspective.

A rare objective view was presented in a very small sidebar accompanying an article in *Newsweek*. It was a short tabulation of fatalities from various causes in 1985:

According to the magazine, 25 Americans were killed by terrorists worldwide in that year. Meanwhile, there were more than 1,300 homicides in New York City alone. The magazine contained the information that 1985 also saw 3,000 deaths by drowning in the United States, 50,000 killed in car accidents, and other equally grim statistics.

Obviously, foreign travel is not one of our more dangerous pursuits, but the unbalanced media coverage, and the resulting distorted public perceptions, played havoc for a time with my airline and my job.

Whole batteries of new security procedures have since been put into place in an effort to convince terrorists that civilian airliners are no longer easy targets. Getting aboard airplanes is more inconvenient now, but once past the watchful eyes of the security forces, we have every confidence of peacefully flying our passengers to the destination shown in the timetable, and international travel is returning to normal levels.

Do you have nightmares or trouble sleeping at night?

No. I can understand how this behavior pattern would appear in people who have substituted trust in self or in any human institution for trust in God. Trust in self is fine until one is overwhelmed by events. Then confidence evaporates and negatives such as fear, anger, and panic take over. Even if the outcome is satisfactory, the trauma leaves psychological damage that may or may not heal.

I had learned long ago that God's promises are absolutely trustworthy if I place my affairs in His care and keeping—and that King David's words are as apropos today as they were three thousand years ago:

". . . in God I trust; I will not be afraid. What can mortal man do to me?" (Psalms 56:4 NIV.)

Since there was no terror at the time, there has been no trauma since.

What should we do to combat hijacking and terrorism?

In the short-term, we are on the right track. Airline security has been tightened to military levels and civilian airliners are no longer easy targets for cause promoters of every persuasion.

International travel is more inconvenient now, but much safer. We are determined to stop violence directed at innocent travelers, just like the shotgun riders of a century ago who rode the Western stagecoaches.

However, it is important to recognize that many of the militant terrorists now coming out of the Middle East have no resemblance whatever to old-time highwaymen, aside from their method of operation.

Typically, their ransom demand is for the release of compatriots held in some prison or other, a concept that would have drawn only a blank look from Jesse James.

They have been described by our government officials as thugs, cowards, and hoodlums, but banditry of this type does not commit suicide in order to achieve its ends. A more accurate comparison would be to the World War II Japanese kamikaze pilots. The actions of both are alien to the Western mind, but there are tremendous similarities, especially with regard to intensity of allegiance to a purpose.

To misread your opponent's motivations and commitment is to tie one hand behind your back in dealing with him. In trying to understand the complex problems in the Middle East, it is tempting to simplify by labeling opponents as common criminals and to use standard law-enforcement measures in efforts to keep the peace.

The major weakness in this approach is that, on a practical level, it probably will not work. If motivation is deep enough, human ingenuity will find ways to defeat any defensive system. Israel is a good example of this. An armed camp, it is the foremost champion of stern punishment and swift retribution, yet its citizens are no safer now than they were forty years ago. On a moral level, it ignores the possibility that there might be some justification for the violence and anger of the terrorists and denies the opportunity to do something positive about it.

As it is, our protective measures are similar to Band-Aids covering the symptoms. They are intended to give the appearance that all is well, while ignoring the underlying disease.

Before the hijacking I was like most Americans in that I really had no idea what was happening in the political arena in the Middle East and had very little understanding of what the various groups wanted. I was awakened from this typically American isolation by the black bore of an automatic pistol in my face and by the angry eyes behind it.

The forced confinement that followed led me and my fellow captives to look around us with keen interest in an effort to find out just what was going on. In my case, this interest continued, and I have discovered that if we want to point fingers and affix blame for the trauma in the Middle East, there's plenty for everyone, including ourselves.

This is disturbing to Americans, especially older ones such as myself. We were raised on Fourth of July parades, developed the feeling that we had won the world's wars and restored peace to the planet, and capped the whole thing off with that triumph of generosity—the Marshall Plan. If the rest of the world did not always share our admirable opinion of ourselves, that was its problem. We were the good guys and we wore our white hats of virtue proudly.

However, our white hats are no longer glistening in the Middle East. They are grimy and tattered.

I have discovered that our country is resented in that region for two primary reasons, one of which is our unfortunate propensity for supporting unsavory regimes of one sort or another. Our support of the Shah of Iran long after he had lost the support of his own people is probably the most unfortunate example of this policy. The Iranian people and the rest of the world are now afflicted with Khomeini and his followers, along with their intense hatred of everything Western and, especially, American.

Another example with which I was directly involved is American support of the Gemayel government in Lebanon. At no time has it enjoyed any popular support. It could not capitalize on massive American aid during our presence there and has had no positive influence in the country since. Gemayel made no moves in our behalf while we were in Beirut, probably because he did not have the means to do so. He remains a block to peace in that shattered country and our support has caused deep resentment toward the United States within the Moslem majority.

The other major cause of resentment toward America in Arab lands is our blind, unquestioning support of Israel and its actions. I have been an admirer of Israel and its people for years, since I first saw the desert blooming under their talented hands. However, the Israelis are human just as we are, and they do make mistakes. In fact, they have made grievous mistakes in that region, and they are not good neighbors.

We are their friends and allies; if we were their true friends we would be saying, "Brother, what you are doing is not right."

President Carter did that in 1978 when he asked for and got a pullback from the first Israeli invasion of Lebanon.

Prime Minister Begin succeeded in his next adventure, the West Bank settlement, and Israel now has to maintain an occupation army in an area that it cannot assimilate, cannot govern properly, and does not care to set free.

Water has been unilaterally diverted from the Jordan River for Israeli irrigation purposes, and this has caused resentment and bitterness among surrounding Arabs which any Southwestern United States farmer would understand.

The most spectacular error was the 1982 invasion of Lebanon, which was roundly condemned everywhere except within official Washington. The Beirut refugee camp massacres were the equal of anything seen in the Nazi Holocaust, yet only vigorous Israeli public outcry prevented a complete cover-up by the Begin government.

Shimon Peres has said that the invasion of Lebanon was a grievous mistake because it let the Shi'ite genie out of the bottle—that in all the years they had fought the Palestine Liberation Organization, Israel had never seen one terrorist turn himself into a human bomb. Israel went into Lebanon to destroy one enemy but its harshness created the hate that resulted in a worse one.

This same hate is directed at our government because it is deemed to be as one with Israel.

Syrian President Assad has said, "The United States does not have an independent opinion or an American policy in this region. The United States implements the policy that is decided by Israel."

A similar thought was echoed by the young Amal captain when he asked me why the United States did not restrain Israel in its invasion of Lebanon. I remembered the massive public outcry that had erupted in this country at the time, but I said to him, "We can't conduct another country's foreign policy."

"Come now, Captain," he had said, laughing at my response. "You are the mightiest superpower on earth, and little Israel is totally dependent upon you. You paid for this invasion. You cannot tell them how to spend your money?"

Had President Reagan followed President Carter's example and stopped the invasion when it began, he could have prevented a good deal of the grief that has come to us and the Israelis since then.

If they know the facts of a given situation, Americans generally respond in a fair and compassionate manner. However, we have received a distorted, biased picture of events in the Middle East, and our perceptions and responses have been distorted as a result.

In the Middle East as everywhere else, there are two sides to the story. When we focus only on our own grievances it ensures that the violence and the terrorism will continue indefinitely.

We need to be very firm in our measures dealing with violence against innocent citizens, but we also need to be fair in our dealings with all the people in the Middle East. The United States should once again return to the doctrine of an evenhanded policy there. Our actions of some years back may or may not have matched our rhetoric, but in any event airliners were not attacked and America was not perceived as a malignant evil.

A perception that the United States is addressing legitimate grievances fairly and working to eliminate injustice and oppression wherever they are found will go a long way toward defueling the engine of hate that is directed against us.

If a young man sees that he can get a job, get married and support his family, have a decent amount of self-respect, and manage his own affairs, he is not likely to live in the trenches and throw bombs at innocent people. Then crazies such as Khadafy will not have the manpower base to support their schemes and will be as easily contained as any other crackpot.

If God's way of understanding, consideration, and communication replaces man's way of strike and counterstrike we will no longer have to worry about some new form of terrorism hitting us unexpectedly, and I will once again be able to safely fly my passengers back and forth across the Mediterranean.

251

SUGGESTED READING

For those interested in doing further research into conditions in the Middle East, I recommend the following books:

All Fall Down, by Gary Sick (Random House, 1985). This is a detailed accounting of the Iranian hostage crisis as seen by the assistant to the national security advisor.

Bloodbrothers, by David Hazard and Elias Chacour (Chosen Books, 1984) presents insights into the establishment of Israel in Palestine. The author is an Arab Christian, at first a refugee who later returned to Israel as a Christian pastor to minister to his people. The title refers to the relationship between Arab and Jew.

Sacred Rage, by Robin Wright (Simon and Schuster, 1985). This book gives an accurate in-depth analysis of the rise of militant Islam across the Middle East. Wright is an investigative reporter working out of Beirut.

The Blood of Abraham, by Jimmy Carter (Houghton-Mifflin, 1985). A careful examination of events, both historic and current, that affect conditions in the Middle East.

Some Events in Lebanon Leading up to the Hijacking of TWA Flight 847

1982—Israeli forces invade southern Lebanon to strike against PLO bases there. The Israelis are originally welcomed by the inhabitants of Southern Lebanon, but their "iron-fist" policy soon turns the populace against them.

1983—United States Marines enter Beirut as part of a multinational peace-keeping force.

September 19, 1983—The *U.S.S. Virginia* shells Druse forces in defense of the beleaguered Lebanese Army, thus costing the United States its appearance of neutrality. The action is protested by the marine commander in Beirut as an extreme danger to the safety of his troops.

October 23, 1983—A suicide bomber demolishes the U.S. Marine barracks in Beirut, killing 241 marines.

1984—Early in the year, the battleship *New Jersey* shells Moslem Beirut and its suburbs, violently intensifying anti-American feeling.

September 6, 1984—The United States vetoes a United Nations resolution condemning Israel's tactics in Lebanon.

September 20, 1984—The U.S. Embassy annex in East Beirut is destroyed by a suicide bomber, and the American forces begin to pull out of Lebanon.

March 8, 1985—A car bomb attack is made on the Beirut home of Sheikh Fadlallah, a well-known and influential Lebanese cleric. He is not killed in the attack, but CIA involvement is rumored and widely reported in the city.

February to June 1985—Israel pulls out of Lebanon, taking several hundred Shi'ite hostages as security for their departing troops. Instead of releasing the prisoners when their withdrawal is complete, the Israelis move them to Atlit prison camp in northern Israel.

June 14, 1985—TWA Flight 847 is hijacked by Shi'ite gunmen who are seeking release of the prisoners being held by Israel.

June 30, 1985—American hostages are released, followed by release of the Shi'ite hostages held at the Atlit camp.